72 12.00

PURNELL LIBRARY OF KNOWLEDGE

The Wonderful Story of the Jews

SBN 361 01538 0
First published in 1970 by PURNELL, London
© 1970 by B.P.C. Publishing Limited, London
Printed in Italy

THE WONDERFUL STORY OF THE JEWS

by Plantagenet Somerset Fry, F.R.S.A.
Foreword by Dr. Jacob Gewirtz
Literary Editor of the Jewish Chronicle

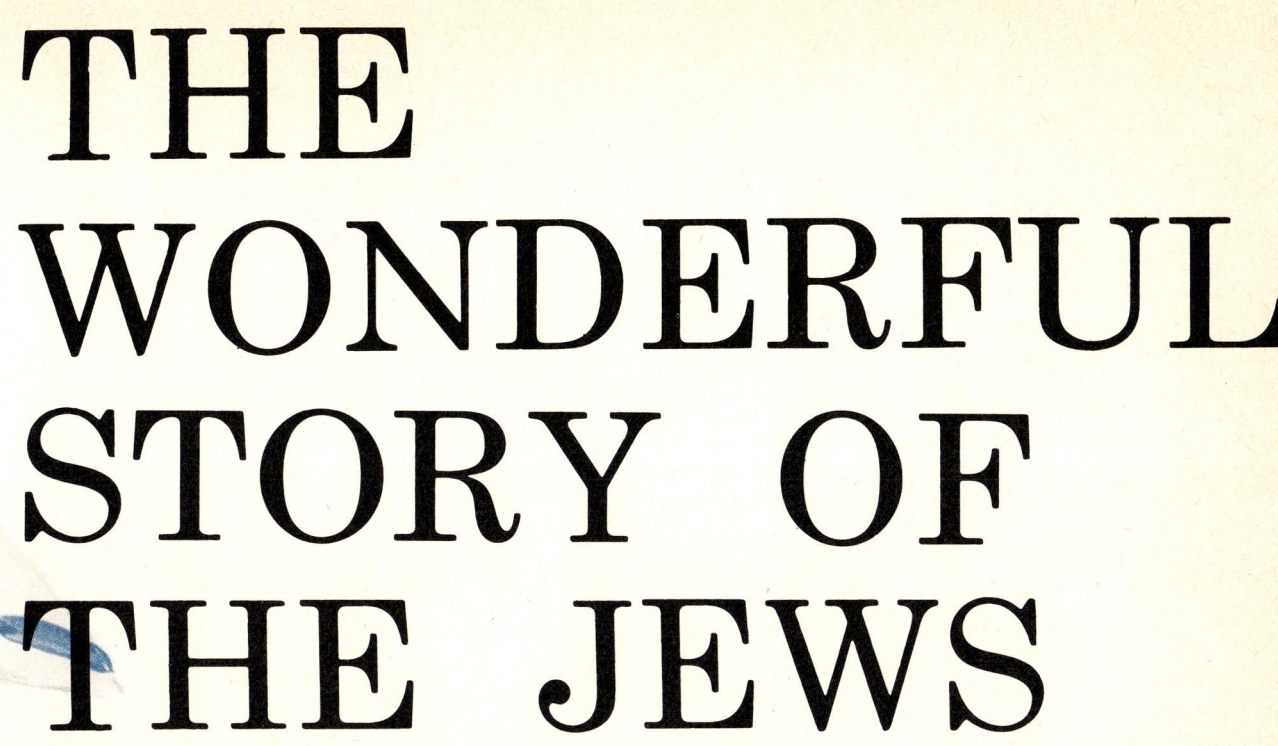

PURNELL
London

Foreword

by Jacob Gewirtz

Despite the enormous outpourings of books, newspaper articles and learned dissertations on the Jews and their history, this ancient people still remains an enigma to a sizeable segment of their fellow men. This is understandable, for the annals of Jewish History are fraught with contradictions. Chosen by God to lead the nations of the world to universal peace, brotherhood and justice, they are themselves subjected to the unending ravages of war, persecution and tyranny. Heirs to the Promised Land of milk and honey they are forced to traverse the face of the earth for 2,000 years homeless and rootless. Indeed, their very survival as a people after disasters that have obliterated mightier nations – Phoenicians, Assyrians, Hittites and Hun – is a mystery that has yet to be unravelled by philosophers and historians. Nor is there agreement even among Jews upon a fundamental definition of the word "Jew". Is he a member of a race, religion, nation or cultural group? Even in Israel where important legal consequences await a definite answer to this perplexing question there has been no final determination. It would be unfair to expect the author of the book you are about to read to provide you with the answer. It is enough that in his admirable attempt to compress 4,000 years of history into 92 pages, Somerset Fry has amply succeeded in stimulating the reader to pursue the subject further.

History is more than a ledger of names, events and dates. Nor is it merely a compendium of the lives of great men. Moses, Jesus, Einstein and Freud were all Jews but they are not the sum total of Jewish experience. Historians, of necessity, are forced to concentrate on the unusual, the extraordinary, the exotic. Jewish history as you will see in the pages that follow is resplendent with moments of glorious triumph. More often it is the blood-stained record of man's inhumanity to man. If there is a simple lesson that we can learn from the history of the Jews it is that before we can begin to love our neighbour we must first try to understand him.

Contents

Foreword	8
The Children of Israel	10
Abraham and His Family	10
The Hebrews in Egypt	12
Moses and the Exodus	14
Return to Canaan	16
The Heroic Days	18
A Judge and a King	18
David	20
Solomon	22
Two Kingdoms	24
The Fall of Israel and Judah	26
Rebellions and Survival	28
Under the Persians and the Greeks	28
The Maccabees	30
Subject to the Romans	32
Herod the Great	34
The Beginning of the End	36
A Time of Reformers	36
Jesus of Nazareth	38
Defeat for Rome	40
The Fall of Jerusalem	42
The Patriarchs	44
The Diaspora	46
The Jews and Islam	46
The Jews in Moslem Spain	48
Jewish Philosophers of the Middle Ages	50
The Hill of Darkness	52
Persecution Begins in Europe	52
The Jews in England	54
The First Expulsions	56
Toleration in Poland	58
Defence of the Faith	59
Spain—Inquisition and Expulsion	60
The Ghettos	62
The Dawn of Liberty	64
The Jews Go to the East	64
Marranos and the Age of Discovery	66
Holland Helps the Jews	68
A Famous Philosopher	70
The Burden Begins to be Lifted	72
The Jews in France	74
The Struggle for Equal Rights	76
Jews in the 19th Century	76
The Jews in America	78
The Beginning of Zionism	80
The Balfour Declaration	82
Tragedy and Liberation	84
Palestine in the 1930's	84
The Greatest Crime in History	86
The Creation of the State of Israel	88
War with the Arabs	90
The Struggle to Preserve Nationhood	91
Index	93

The Children of Israel

This is a drawing of a small Sumerian priest-god figure from the area around the city of Ur, probably dated about 2250-2040 B.C. The little statuette is wearing typical robes and headdress of the time.

Below is a drawing after an ancient mosaic showing Abraham and Sarah.

Abraham and his Family

THE story of the Jews began over four thousand years ago. Then, in what is often called the Fertile Crescent, the land around the rivers Tigris and Euphrates, two important civilizations had been flourishing for a long time. The Sumerian civilization was the first in all history, and the other, the Babylonian, had grown up alongside the Sumerian.

In and around the Fertile Crescent dwelt many other races in varying stages of development. Among these were the Semitic races, people who probably came originally from Arabia. The word Semitic describes the group of languages which these people spoke. Some Semites had settled in Sumer, or had been brought there after wars or raiding expeditions. Some of the earliest Semites belonged to a tribe living near the city of Ur, whose chief (in the twentieth century B.C.) was a man called Abraham.

This tribe appears to have grown tired of life under the Sumerians and decided to leave in search of new land to begin a fresh life. Abraham led them out of Sumer into Syria and down into the Hebron district of Canaan, approximately the area known as Israel today. These early Semites came to be called Hebrews and there they continued their life of sheep farming and crop growing.

Abraham understood the laws in Ur and he attempted to introduce legal principles in Canaan. For example, lands were properly paid for and transfer deeds prepared. No doubt many of Abraham's ideas formed the background to the laws which Moses set out hundreds of years later, although Moses said they were the laws of God.

Mention of God brings us to one of the most interesting things about the Hebrews. They were the first known people in the world to worship only one God. Other early civilizations had a large assortment of gods and goddesses to represent such things as the earth, the sky, the sun, the water and the moon. But Abraham's people recognized only one supreme being, a deity YHWH, which later generations referred to as Yahweh or Jahweh.

Abraham went further and signified his people as God's chosen people in a number of ways. One of these was a custom that all male babies should have a small operation called circumcision. Another was the abolition of human sacrifice.

Abraham and his family remained in Canaan for many years. According to the Old Testament, Abraham's son was Isaac, and Isaac's son was Jacob, whose other name was Israel. Isaac and Jacob may have been leaders of the Hebrews rather than members of Abraham's family, but they were no doubt related.

Jacob had twelve sons, who in their time became leaders of twelve Hebrew tribes in Canaan. They were known as the "Children of Israel." Their names were Reuben, Simeon, Levi, Judah, Dan, Naphtali, Gad, Asher, Issachar, Zebulun, Joseph and Benjamin.

The map shows the Fertile Crescent between the Tigris and Euphrates rivers. There the Sumerian and Babylonian civilizations grew up. From the city of Ur, Abraham and his people began the journey to the Promised Land of Canaan.

The coloured areas show the nations according to the book of Genesis in the Bible. Gomer was inhabited by the descendants of Japheth, Ophir was inhabited by Shem's descendants, and in Lubim the descendants of Ham lived.

Shem, Ham and Japheth were the three sons of Noah and, by tradition, it was their children and their children's children who peopled the Middle Eastern area after the Great Flood.

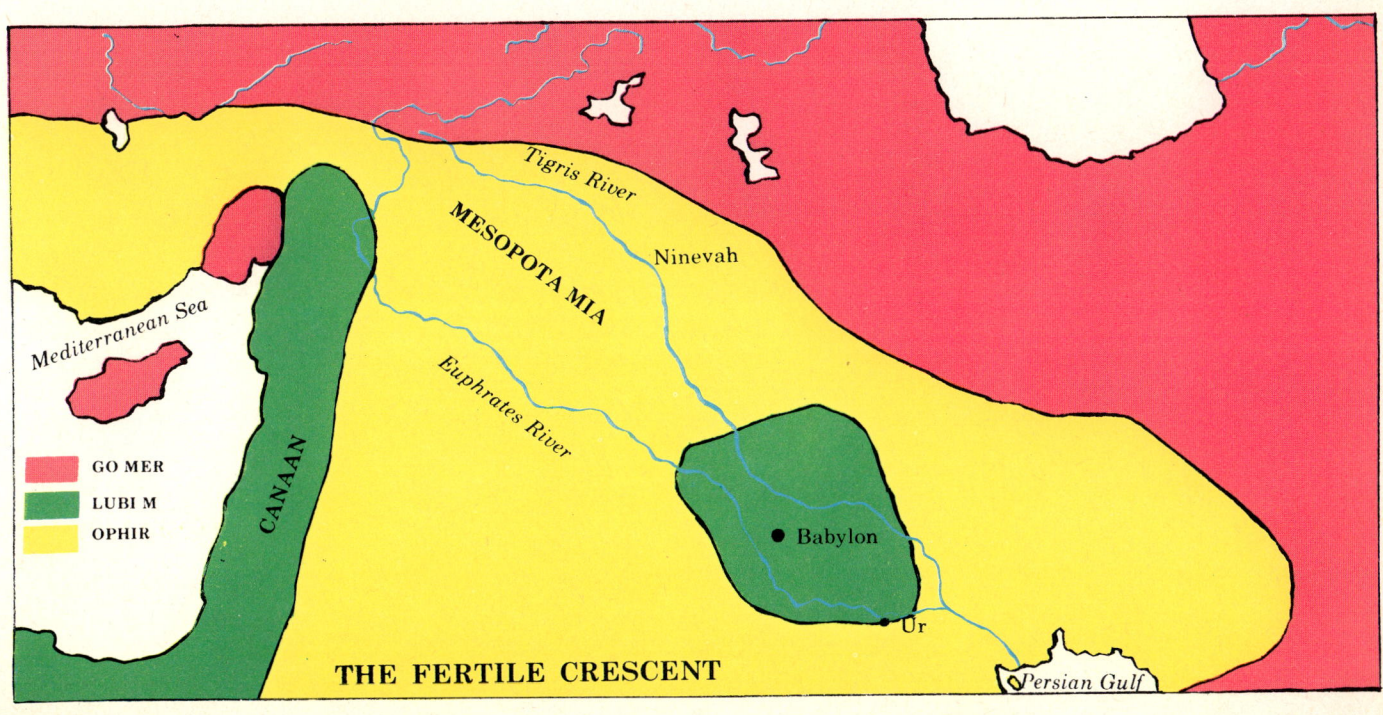

The Hebrews in Egypt

THERE is not much rain in Canaan and crop-growing was very difficult. From time to time, the Hebrews endured harsh famines. Some more enterprising Hebrews left Canaan and wandered to Egypt to the northern end of the Nile where the lands were much more fertile.

Among them was Joseph, one of the twelve sons of Jacob, who the Old Testament tells us was sold as a slave to the Egyptians. Whether or not this was so, Joseph grew up to be a man of some importance in the Egyptian government, and he acted as economic adviser to the Pharaoh for a while.

Gradually the Hebrews settled down in the Nile Delta and because of their skills and abilities were accepted, and even welcomed, by the Egyptians.

In about 1750 B.C. Egypt, which had developed its civilization over two thousand years or more for the most part unhindered by neighbouring

> **Sukkoth**
> *The Feast of the Tabernacles, Sukkoth, is the ancient festival of thanksgiving. It celebrates the coming of autumn and the late harvest. In the book of Leviticus in the Old Testament, God commands Moses that His people shall celebrate, for seven days, His protection of them during their wandering in the wilderness. During this festival, booths (or tabernacles) are prepared in the open air and covered with branches so that the stars can be seen through the roofs. Each booth is gaily decorated with a rich array of fruits and vegetables, and meals are eaten within. A blessing is said before each meal, "Blessed art Thou, O Lord... Who has commanded us to dwell in a booth".*

races and empires, was dealt the severest blow of its early history. A well-organized invasion by Semites from Palestine, mingled with Semitic peoples from Arabia, over-ran the whole of Lower Egypt. These invaders were called the Hyksos, a word meaning foreigners. They established a kind of empire in the north, employing some of the Egyptians and expelling the remainder southwards.

The Hyksos were welcomed by the Hebrews already settled in the area. For a while they all prospered, for Egypt was an extremely rich land.

Then in about 1550 B.C. the reigning pharaoh of Upper Egypt, Ahmose I, marshalled a huge army of well-trained and disciplined troops and invaded Lower Egypt. It was a well-planned campaign and it succeeded within a few months. The Hyksos kingdom was overthrown and the Hyksos were expelled.

Neither Ahmose nor the pharaohs before him had overlooked the prosperity the Hebrews had been enjoying in Lower Egypt. Nor did they forget that earlier pharaohs had welcomed the first Hebrews and allowed them to settle in the Nile Delta. So when the Hyksos were driven out, it is understandable that the Pharaoh reserved special punishment for those Hebrews who remained. They were, in fact, to pay the price of kinship.

All Hebrews were deprived of their freedom and wealth and enslaved. One pharaoh actually ordered all their new-born sons to be put to death. The bulk of the Hebrews were forced to work on massive building projects such as the erecting of vast tombs, monuments and palaces.

Occasionally a Hebrew was given slightly better treatment, like being employed in the royal accounts department or in an architect's drawing office, for the Egyptians were sometimes short of skilled professional people. Some Hebrews were allowed to be priests to their own people, but the government of Egypt watched their activities by means of spies and informers, for it did not ignore the possibility that the Hebrews might rebel.

A drawing showing Semitic prisoners in bondage in the land of Egypt.

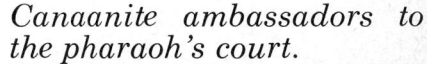

Canaanite ambassadors to the pharaoh's court.

Rameses, the Great, pharaoh of Egypt. Moses asked him to let the Israelites return to their homeland.

The map shows the route Moses and his people travelled on their Exodus from Egypt.

Moses and the Exodus

For centuries the Hebrews had to endure conditions of slavery, but in the thirteenth century B.C. they found a new religious leader, Moses. He had been discovered, abandoned, in a basket of reeds in the Nile and brought up in the Egyptian royal household. When he grew up he became a priest, and decided that the time had come to make a bid for freedom. So he asked the pharaoh, probably Rameses II, to let him take the Hebrews back to the land of Canaan.

At first Rameses refused. Moses thereupon prophesied that the anger of God would be shown in many unpleasant ways. A series of natural disasters occurred, probably by coincidence, such as heavy rains which ruined crops, plagues, and diseases which killed off the fish in the rivers.

One violent plague killed a large number of Egyptian babies. The Hebrew children seemed immune to the disease. It is believed that they were spared because Moses had warned the parents in advance to sacrifice a lamb to God and to spread some of the blood on the front doors of their houses. This was to warn the Messenger of Death that Hebrews dwelt therein, and that he should pass over their houses. Today, Jews all over the world still celebrate a feast called the Passover, every spring.

During the plague Rameses lost a son. This so upset him that he agreed to let the Hebrews leave Egypt. At once Moses assembled his people and gave the signal to begin the great journey back towards Canaan. The event was known as the Exodus.

You can see on the map the approximate route the Hebrews took. This long journey took many years, during which time the travellers were often attacked by desert raiders.

This fresco or wall painting called The Exodus of the Hebrews and the Passage of the Red Sea *was found in the ancient synagogue of Duros-Europus, in Syria. The painting illustrates one of the most famous events in the history of the Jews.*

Rameses ordered an army to pursue Moses and if possible kill him, but the troops were overcome by the desert winds and the heat.

When the Hebrews reached Mount Sinai they settled down for a while. During this interval Moses drew up a series of laws by which the people should be governed if any form of political organization was to survive. This was by no means a new idea. The Sumerians had had laws long before 3000 B.C. as had the Egyptians. The Babylonian king, Hammurabi, had drawn up a code which served as a background for the laws of many succeeding civilizations.

For many years the Hebrews themselves had been developing laws regarding property, business, marriage and many other matters. They had also begun to work out a code of living which governed their whole behaviour towards their fellow human beings. This later came to be called the Torah (the Law).

Moses presented what he believed were the orders of God, the basis of which were embraced by the Ten Commandments. These commandments have governed Jewish—and later Christian—people ever since. Moses also organized the law so that his successors could improve upon it as time went on.

The Passover
The Feast of the Passover is celebrated by Jews in memory of their deliverance from Egypt in the time of Pharaoh Rameses II. It is a feast lasting a week in the spring, and during that time the only bread Jews can eat is matzah, or unleavened bread. Matzah was the bread baked by the Hebrews in the Sinai desert during the Exodus. Wheat flour is mixed with water but without the addition of yeast. When the mixture is baked the loaf is flat, or unleavened.

The Passover celebration begins with a meal which is called the Seder. This is an important meal, and Jews bring out the best silver, china and glass. Care is also taken with the choice of wine.

During the meal the family reads from a special book, the Haggadah, or Passover book. This is a kind of play in which members of the family take parts, and the story is the story of the original Passover.

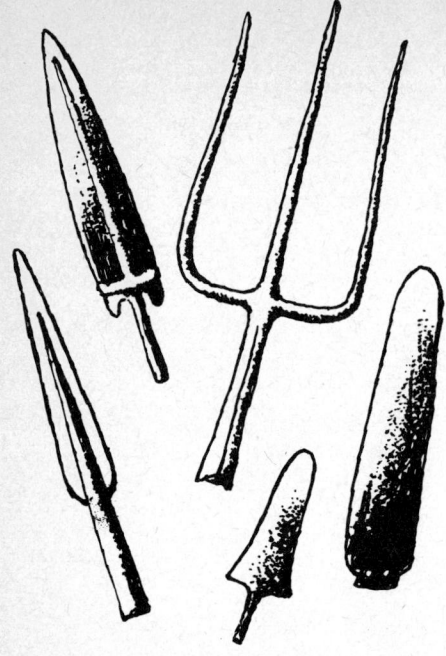

These are examples of the kind of iron tools and weapons made and used by the early Philistines.

Milk and Meat
What Jews eat and drink is regulated by their dietary laws which stem from Biblical times. Some kinds of food are prohibited. These include meat which is regarded as "unclean" in Biblical terms, that is, animals from which the blood has not been extracted by the process of salting. Jews must also not eat meals in which dishes of meat are mixed with products of milk. Nor must they eat fish that have no fins or scales. And they are also not to eat fruit in the year in which it has been picked.

Some of these prohibitions are mentioned in Leviticus, the Third Book of Moses, but it is not clear exactly why such restrictions are intended. It is believed, however, that they are aids to the furtherance of self-discipline. Food that is acceptable is described as kasher, *meaning "fit", and sometimes this word is spelled* kosher.

Return to Canaan

AFTER a while the Hebrews left the Sinai desert and headed for Canaan. Moses did not live to see them reach the "Promised Land", for he died not long after presenting the Ten Commandments, and was greatly mourned. He had been a father-figure for a generation, and had delivered his people from Egyptian bondage.

When the Hebrews got close to the borders of Canaan they began to divide up into tribes, more or less the twelve tribes of Israel, and from then on were known as the Israelites. As soon as they crossed the borders, however, they ran into trouble with the various other tribes living in Canaan. Some of their new enemies were in fact their own kinsmen, descendants of Abraham's people who had not joined the emigration to Egypt centuries earlier.

Chief among the enemies of the Israelites were

the Philistines, a warlike people who occupied fortified cities along the Palestine coast of the Mediterranean below Mount Carmel. These Philistines had iron weapons and tools, and continually raided Canaan and other territories.

On the whole, however, the Israelite occupation of Canaan was a peaceful one. They found that the Canaanites had badly neglected their farms because they did not know how to obtain and distribute water in dry weather. So the Israelites introduced the technique of collecting rain water and storing it in large tanks, so that it could be used when needed. Soon the whole land began to prosper, and before long excited the envy of her neighbours.

Having solved their agricultural problems and established small industries, the Israelites began to develop a system of government, following the principles of Moses. Each of the tribes was more or less independent but was governed along common lines under one system of law. The tribes elected assemblies to act as governing bodies. These later came to be known as sanhedrins (*See* page 35).

The Israelites built few cities, and preferred to live as country folk centred round a sprinkling of well managed farms. Although they now enjoyed a prosperity their ancestors had not known in Abraham's days, they had to work very hard. This made them tough, and it also made them virtuous. They had little opportunity for enjoying themselves in the sort of luxuries and idle pleasures that prevailed in Egypt or Babylon.

It was not long before the Israelites clashed with their Philistine neighbours. From time to time these aggressive people invaded Israel because they regarded the Israelites as a danger to their peace and stability. Quite often the Israelites were defeated and farms were burned and treasures stolen. A respite was won when the Israelites produced a leader like Samson, who could outmanoeuvre the Philistine army or defeat it in battle. But victories could not have any lasting effect until the Israelites learned the value of unity as a people.

Philistine warriors in their battle dress.

The Heroic Days

The priest and judge Samuel chose Saul to be king.

A Torah ark—the handsomely decorated case which houses the scrolls of Hebrew law. From ancient times to the present the Torah has always been kept in an ark. Synagogues have Torah scrolls encased in an ark.

A Judge and a King

THE struggle with the Philistines was not the only problem for the Israelites. Attacks, often severe and prolonged, came from other quarters. There were times when Israel was pressed on all sides, by the Moabites, the Edomites, the Midianites and the Ammonites. All had highly-trained mounted warriors. Territory on the borders changed hands often and some of the people living there probably did not always know who their masters were.

Eventually the Israelites realized that they needed to have permanent defence. This could only be achieved by a new system of government which would provide leadership for all the tribes. Soon, there was a strong movement among Israelites urging the creation of a monarchy.

They had been governed by elected assemblies for some time, and they had also looked for leadership from their war chiefs, whom they called "judges". The judges came to be accepted as the leading men of the tribes, but their influence and power was not passed on to their sons.

One of the last judges was Samuel. While he saw the need for a hereditary succession of leadership, he argued that it should apply to the judges themselves. The people did not agree. They wished to start afresh, and they asked him to "anoint a King unto us". This meant finding a suitable candidate and having him properly crowned with all due ceremony. (Anointing a king meant putting special oil upon his head to signify that he was chosen by God. This particular ceremony has survived ever since the days of Samuel in many parts of the world where monarchies still exist.)

Samuel looked around and found a tall, thick-set, courageous and purposeful man called Saul. He was a farmer from the tribe of Benjamin, but he had

This drawing shows how Saul may have looked. His battle dress is typical of the period in which he lived.

outstanding qualities of leadership. His shyness and reserve helped to give him the reputation of being a somewhat unusual person.

Saul was anointed the first king of Israel, in about 1025 B.C. As it was the first crowning ceremony (or coronation, as we call it now), it must have been a splendid affair, for the Israelites were not poor and probably welcomed Saul as the leader they needed.

In making Saul king, Samuel imagined that he would be able to maintain his own power as the leading judge and continue to influence the course of events in Israel. Samuel was proved to be wrong. Saul was a man of great strength of mind, and determined once he was in a high position to rule properly and, if necessary, sternly.

David

King David was by no means just a soldier and statesman. He was also a man of artistic and intellectual gifts. As a young man his skill in harp-playing attracted the attention of King Saul who invited him to court. Quite probably David composed poetry at this time. And certainly when he was king, David did write some very fine songs. Some of these are in the Book of Psalms, in the Old Testament.

THE Israelites had the king they sought, but in some respects Saul proved to be a disappointment. He did not lack courage in battle, but he missed chances of surprising the enemy and so was sometimes caught himself. At home, although he began some reforms in the governing of the people, he quarrelled with the judges. Samuel was distressed that Saul did not use him as chief adviser, and attempted to win the loyalty of the king's son-in-law, David. Samuel even secretly anointed David as successor to Saul.

The king was extremely angry. On one occasion when he and David had led an army against an enemy, beaten it, and returned home to Israel, and the welcoming cheers seemed to be especially for David, Saul decided his son-in-law must be kept in his place. David, however, fled from court stirring up the tribes against the king.

David was driven out of Israel and took refuge with the Philistines. Recognizing his abilities, the Philistines invited him to take part in further expeditions against Israel. Before David could decide to help the Philistines, they attacked Israel, and defeated and killed Saul and many of his sons during a great battle. The Philistines annexed a considerable part of Israel.

Thinking they had won David over to their cause, the Philistines appointed him king of the annexed territory. This was to spell their ruin.

David was the type of leader the Hebrews needed. He was a brave soldier, a popular leader of men, a subtle politician, and greatly interested in, if not always devoted to, law-making and religion.

To begin with David built up a standing army, something the Israelites had not had before. He reorganized the government, filling the top positions with people in whom ability counted for more than wealth or background.

David created a national capital almost right in the heart of Israel, at Jerusalem. The city was on the top of a hill and could be seen from many miles away. There he erected buildings as magnificent as those in Egyptian, Babylonian and Phoenician cities.

In battles David had enormous success. He defeated the Ammonites, the Edomites and the Aramaeans. They all paid tribute, thus enriching Israel's treasury. He turned on the Philistines and dealt them a blow from which they never recovered.

By the end of David's long reign, Israel dominated land that stretched from Sinai in the south to Syria in the north, including almost the whole coastline from Gaza to Sidon. He had created a strong central government, and at the same time given some powers to regional governors in the provinces. The reign of David was one of the greatest eras in the history of the Jews.

> **Jerusalem**
> *The city of Jerusalem has always been considered a holy city—by Jews, by Christians, by Moslems and by other religious groups. The name Jerusalem comes from the city's ancient pre-Israelite name, Urusalim, and means "City of Safety or Peace". The city has been called the "bride of kings and the mother of prophets". In a history spanning thirty-three centuries, Jerusalem has been destroyed by earthquakes, razed by invaders, has survived twenty sieges and blockades, undergone eighteen reconstructions and two periods of complete desolation, and passed six times from one religion to another. Still the city thrives in modern times—a focal point between the East and the West. Jerusalem is the seat of the government of Israel today.*

Solomon

David died in about 970 B.C. and his son Solomon, who earned a reputation for being very rich and very wise, became king.

Solomon was in many ways as clever and as successful as his father. He was an able military leader, yet built up alliances with his neighbours rather than going to war with them. This he did either by arranging marriages between royal families (he married an Egyptian princess) or by drawing up trade pacts which brought benefits to both sides. For example, he signed a treaty with the Phoenicians and encouraged some of their craftsmen and artists to work in Jerusalem and other places. He co-operated with the King of Tyre to mine gold in southern Israel and to share the profits.

Much of the wealth which came from these arrangements was used by Solomon in his great building programme. By far the most important building was a temple for Jerusalem. This followed a promise made by his father to give the people a splendid new place for the worship of God. The huge building took nearly fifteen years to construct. It was adorned with priceless ornaments of gold, silver and precious stones, many made by Phoenician craftsmen.

Solomon also proposed that the new Jerusalem should be a fitting capital for the extended Israelite kingdom, and this meant improving the whole city.

In Jerusalem Solomon entertained foreign monarchs, chief ministers, and commanders-in-chief, sometimes in the company of his friend, the King of Tyre. The banquets, entertainments, and displays became famous throughout the Middle East, much to the alarm of the elders and the priests. The Israelites were not as a rule given to indulging in such worldly luxuries. In some ways, Solomon seemed to be betraying the virtues that had seen the Hebrews through their long ordeals since the

The picture, below, *is a reconstruction of the Temple in Solomon's time.*

days of Abraham and the wandering in the wilderness.

Although it was a splendid age for Israel, the luxuries had to be paid for, and Solomon inflicted very heavy taxation upon the people. He organized taxes on a regional basis, so that richer regions paid more than poorer ones, but the taxes were harsh and the poor naturally resented the whole business.

In about 930 B.C. Solomon died. Within a few years his great kingdom was split in half.

Above: *Trading caravans from all over the Middle East brought beautiful clothing, furnishings, exotic foods and a rich array of treasures to Solomon's court.*

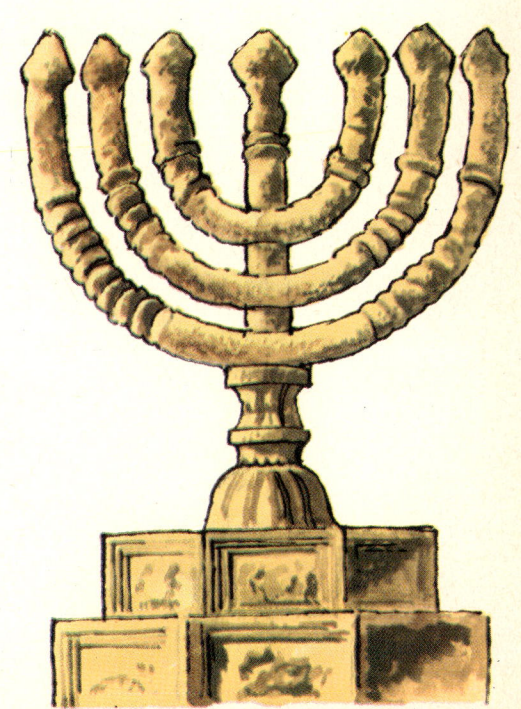

Menorah
Menorah is the Hebrew word for a special type of candlestick which was very famous in early Jewish history. The candlestick, or candelabrum, usually had seven candle holders, in a straight line. There was a famous golden menorah in the Temple at Jerusalem in A.D. 70. The Roman general Titus removed it and took it to Rome after the fall of the city. When an arch was constructed in the Forum at Rome to celebrate Titus' exploits, a menorah was included as a carving on the arch.

Opposite: *Drawings of relics from King Ahab's House of Ivory. Ahab's wife, Jezebel, brought priests of the pagan gods Baal and Ashera to Jewish territory. The prophet, Elisha, who succeeded the great Elijah, determined to bring an end to the royal line of Ahab because of the King's wife's conduct and because she had encouraged Israelite youths to abandon their faith for pagan cults.*
Left: *The Lion Seal of Shema, who was minister to King Jeroboam I.*

Below: *A stele (upright stone pillar) of the Pharaoh Merenptah (c. 1223 B.C.) which is the first mention of the Israelites in contemporary records. The stele records: "Israel is desolate, her seed is not."*

Two Kingdoms

THE death of Solomon marked the beginning of the decline of Israelite power. His son Rehoboam continued the policy of heavy taxation and before long a civil war began. Some of the tribes who had always resented the central government rebelled and the kingdom was divided into two unequal and independent parts.

The smaller kingdom, which extended from Mizpah to Beersheba, was called Judah, from which the word Jew was eventually derived. Rehoboam stayed on as king of Judah, but although its capital was Jerusalem, the kingdom was small, poor and without influence.

The larger kingdom Israel, in the north, had a new capital at Samaria, and included Galilee, central Palestine and Transjordan. Its southernmost city was Jericho, and its first king was Jeroboam, who continued to hold court in Solomon's luxurious style.

The new Israel began to develop into precisely the kind of kingdom it had been formed to oppose. The kings ruled as absolutely as Solomon, but not so well. Jereboam went so far as to introduce the worship of idols, a practice strictly forbidden in the Ten Commandments.

The wealth of the Israelites and their obvious

aptitude in all kinds of trade and business created envy in neighbouring countries, particularly in Egypt. There is evidence that the Egyptians tried to foster bad relations between the two Israelite kingdoms, thus weakening their resources.

The kingdoms, in fact, remained separated, despite prophets and thinkers in both who urged reunification. During the first years of the divided kingdom scholars began to put down in writing the early story of the Hebrews, their development, their laws, their learning. These writings came to form the earlier part of the Old Testament, which was added to as time went by. (Much of what is written in the Old Testament has been proven true by archaeologists' excavations in the past two centuries and confirmed by ancient writings from neighbouring lands.)

The most important people, in these developing times, were the prophets. The word prophet meant more than just a man who could foretell the future. Prophets were usually clear and eloquent writers and speakers, who felt responsible for the conduct of the Jews. They felt that they should help the people to live by the Torah and the laws of Moses. The prophets were not always popular. Some entered politics and attempted to dictate to the kings how they should govern the country or which foreign policy to pursue. Others were persecuted for their interference in people's lives.

In the ninth century B.C. an Israelite noble, Omri, seized power in Israel. His son, Ahab (who married Jezebel, the daughter of the king of Tyre) was an extremely able commander in the field of battle. In about 855 B.C., he marched eastwards against the Assyrian empire leading an army of Phoenicians, Israelites, Philistines and others, and defeated the Assyrians in a great battle at Qarqar.

After Ahab's death the Israelite kingdom began to decline as the old habit of tribal quarrelling revived. There were no leaders strong enough to prevent it. This so weakened the state that a century or so later it was ripe for conquest by the Assyrians.

An artist's conception of what King Sargon II must have looked like.

The Fall of Israel and Judah

In the middle of the eighth century B.C. the Assyrian King, Sargon II, decided the time had come to crush Israel. Although weak, Israel was still very rich, and Israelite merchants dominated the trade routes across Syria, Phoenicia and even into Asia Minor.

Sargon assembled his army and set forth. The Assyrian army was the finest and toughest in the world at the time. The soldiers were armed with iron weapons and equipped with swift chariots which were used in groups as shock forces. Even if the Israelites had been well-disciplined and properly prepared and led, they would probably not have been able to withstand the Assyrians for long. As it was, the Israelite forces were swept back across Israel by the mighty king who rolled into Samaria. After besieging the city for three years, the Assyrians razed it to the ground.

The Israelite leaders, together with many of their people, were deported to distant parts of the empire. The ten main tribes of Hebrews were dispersed and have been regarded as "lost" to history.

Meanwhile, what of Judah? Sargon did not attack the smaller kingdom, perhaps because he considered it unimportant. So Judah survived for more than a century. But the kingdom's days were numbered.

In 613 B.C. the Assyrian empire was brought to a sudden end when the capital, Nineveh, was besieged and, surprisingly, captured by a combined force of Persians and Babylonians.

In 586 the Babylonian king, Nebuchadnezzar II, invaded Judah and captured Jerusalem. The great temple of Solomon was demolished, along with many other public buildings. The Jewish leaders and upper classes were deported to Babylon where they were stripped of their ranks and forced into slavery.

For fifty years the kingdom of Judah consisted

of little more than a collection of peasant farmers who were allowed to work their land. City life almost vanished, and there was no more central government. The kingdom's affairs rested in the hands of a high commissioner. Many Jews were deported to Egypt for hard labour.

In Babylon, meanwhile, the Jews were second-class citizens, but they never gave up hope of returning to Palestine. One of their prophets, Ezekiel, addressed large gatherings on many occasions. He gave them encouragement when he forecast that the power of Babylon would soon give way to that of Persia.

Cyrus the Great, king of Persia, invaded and conquered Babylon in about 540 B.C. thus bringing to an end the Babylonian empire. One of the first acts of the great ruler was to allow the enslaved Judeans, whose spirit and faith had been kept alive by their prophets, to return to their own land. The country was to remain part of the Persian empire, but Cyrus gave the Jews a large measure of self-government. He was careful to select his governor-general from the ranks of the Jews, and he did not interfere with the Jewish religion, its festivals, its worship, or its hierarchy of priests. In this, Cyrus was carrying out the policy the Persians usually adopted towards the lands they conquered.

Nebuchadnezzar, King of Babylon, invaded Judah and when Israel and Judah fell, the Jews were taken in captivity to Babylon.

This stone relief from the Palace of Ashurbanipal of Assyria shows a Judaean being driven into captivity.

Rebellions and Survival

Under the Persians and the Greeks

THE exiles were pleased to be able to return to their home. But they found conditions there had considerably altered. When the Assyrians and the Babylonians had deported the populations of Israel and Judah, neighbours began to move in to the abandoned areas. Here and there they clashed with the farmers who had been allowed to remain. The exiles thus found a variety of peoples living in Palestine.

The Jewish farmers welcomed the exiles with joy, for among them were lawyers, nobles and prophets who could restore order and nationhood to Judah.

But the other peoples were not so friendly. The worst enemies were the Samaritans, who lived in the land surrounding Samaria, once the old capital of Israel. These people were a mixture of Israelite, Assyrian and other Middle East tribes, who had attempted to adopt the Jewish religion. The Jews resented this strongly.

Soon after their return in 538 B.C. the Jews decided to rebuild the temple, but it was not finished until after the Persian king, Darius, had given the money to ensure its completion. It was dedicated at a splendid ceremony in 515 B.C. At the same time much of the old city of Jerusalem was rebuilt.

A drawing from an old woodcut showing the Jews returning from the exile in Babylon to Jerusalem. Below: A copy of a Renaissance painting of Queen Esther. Below opposite: A beautiful Megillah Esther, or the Scroll of Queen Esther read during the celebration of Purim.

Purim

Purim is celebrated by Jews in the spring, about a month before the Christian Easter festival. The festival commemorates the successful foiling of a plot to murder all Jews in Persia in about 480 B.C., organized by the Persian king's chief adviser, Haman.

The king of Persia, Ahasuerus, had married a Jewess, Esther. She had been brought up by a guardian, Mordecai. This worthy man had offended Haman, who in revenge persuaded the king to issue an order that all Jews in Persia should be killed. Haman had a huge gallows erected for Mordecai.

When Esther heard of the danger to her people, and especially to her beloved guardian, she prevailed upon Ahasuerus to cancel the decree. Haman was then arrested and hanged on the gallows built for Mordecai.

Part of the celebrations of Purim used to include hanging an effigy of Haman and burning it.

For the next two hundred years or so the Jews enjoyed a period of relative peace and prosperity, with economic and cultural progress. Under a succession of Persian governors, they developed their own laws and way of life.

Unfortunately they seemed unable to agree among themselves over many things. For example, some regarded "Jewishness" as being a religion, others considered it meant membership of a race of people. Naturally, those who looked upon Jewishness as a religion did not draw the line at admitting other people into the faith, or even marrying outside the faith. This brought its troubles later on. But the Jews learned that laws and customs will survive if they are re-stated time and again. A people whose laws are continually developing to fit the changes of time and status can survive, as a people, if they have no nation or government.

Towards the end of the fourth century B.C. the Macedonian, Alexander the Great, destroyed the Persian empire and conquered lands as far as the borders of India. In the process he took over control of Judah. He also conquered Egypt. This meant that all Jews in the Middle East were under one dominion, although there were differences in beliefs between Jews in Judah, in Egypt and those who had chosen to remain in Babylon at the time of the "Return".

The Jews in Judah welcomed the new regime. Alexander continued the Persian policy of toleration. He encouraged trade, provided fresh outlets for Jewish arts and craftsmanship, and stimulated healthy arguments between Jewish and Greek philosophers and lawyers on legal matters, principles of government and religious matters. This confrontation between Greek and Jewish thinking was important for it lifted Jewish thought and culture on to an international level.

Some time after Alexander's death the early books of the Old Testament were translated into Greek by seventy elders and called the "Septuagint". This spread Jewish ideas far and wide in the Middle East and in areas around the Mediterranean Sea.

A typical High Priest's ceremonial costume.

The Maccabees

WHEN Alexander died his vast empire was split up among his generals. Egypt went to Ptolemy and Syria to Seleucus. Soon the two areas were at loggerheads. Judah along with other states in Palestine lay in between the two areas, and the wrangling forced them to take sides. Some of the Jews were happy with the Ptolemaic rule, others, especially many of the high priests, were in favour of the Seleucid empire.

When the Seleucids expelled the Ptolemies from Judea (in about 198 B.C.), the high priests welcomed the change, for it established that the government of the Jews was bound up with the faith and the priesthood.

The high priests' rule, however, was generally bad. One priest, named Menelaus, was so terrible that in 169 B.C. the people rebelled against him. Menelaus begged aid from the Syrian king, Antiochus IV, who came to Jerusalem, put the revolt down, and allowed his troops to plunder the temple. Menelaus continued to govern even more severely, actually publishing edicts which were contrary to Moses' laws. Within three years a more serious revolt occurred. This time it stemmed from the countryside where the peasantry had been living in conditions far worse than those of the townsfolk. Mattathias, a priest who came from the village of Modin, organised the revolt. Mattathias had been watching the rapid decline of the power of Syria, and had seen the growing strength of Rome (Antiochus was little more than a puppet ruler).

Mattathias lived for only a year after the start of the revolt and its leadership passed to his third son, Judah the Maccabee (Maccabee comes from a word meaning hammer). Judah proved to be a splendid leader, expert in guerilla warfare and ready to share the greatest dangers with his men.

The rebels were not put down because the government could not catch them. In 164 B.C. they attacked Jerusalem and restored the law of Moses.

Judah would accept no titles and would not undertake duties of government. He had restored the law, rejuvenated the faith, and shown Antiochus that he could not trample upon the wishes of the majority. That was what he had set out to do. So he returned to the hills and continued to harass the forces of the Syrian king, but was killed in a skirmish.

Unfortunately, the Maccabean cause was later severely compromised when Judah's brother Jonathan accepted from the Syrian king the ranks and insignia of High Priest and Prince of Judea, which should have been bestowed upon him by the Jews themselves. Doubtless Jonathan believed he was doing it for the good of the people, and certainly he achieved much in his short period of office. When he died mysteriously in about 140 B.C. Judea had grown in strength.

Jonathan's brother Simon succeeded to the position in 142 B.C., but before actually accepting the ranks he put the matter to the assembly of the people in Judea. They voted for him, thereby conferring on him unwisely, as it later proved, absolute power.

Hanukkah

Hanukkah is the name of an eight-day festival to celebrate the victory of Judah the Maccabee over Antiochus IV, the ruler of Syria, in about 165 B.C. It commemorates the fact that Judah had enabled the Jews to go back to their Temple in Jerusalem and clean it up after it had been plundered and desecrated by Antiochus' troops.

When the Temple was under siege in A.D. 70, an oil lamp is said to have burned for eight days. This was regarded as a miracle. To commemorate this a special kind of lamp like a menorah was introduced which had eight branches. The Hanukkah festival was combined with this commemoration of the miracle, and as a result the lamps became known as Hanukkah menorahs.

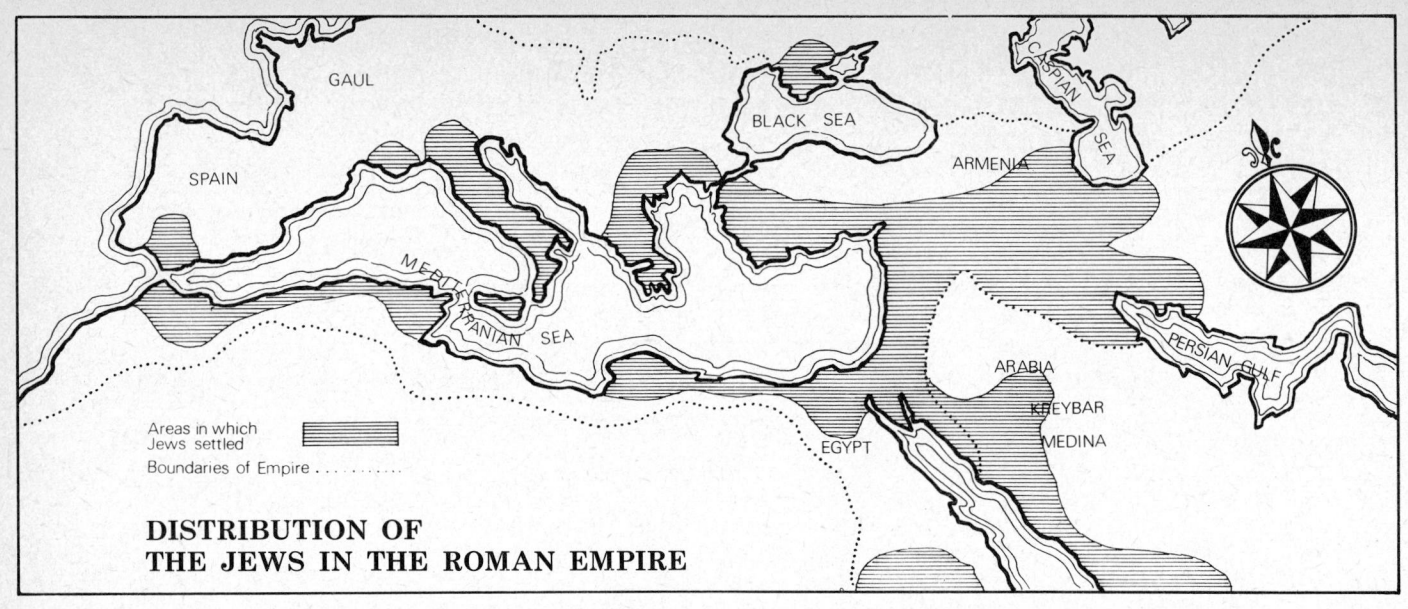

DISTRIBUTION OF
THE JEWS IN THE ROMAN EMPIRE

Subject to the Romans

The map above shows the distribution of the Jews in the Roman Empire. There were large communities of Jews in many major cities of the empire—in Rome, Naples, Genoa, Athens, Alexandria, Damascus, and Antioch, among others.

THE rule of Simon was not popular. He governed in much the same high-handed manner as Menelaus, and things got so bad that some of the leading Jews appealed directly to Rome for a replacement. The Romans responded by appointing their own governor, who was equally unsatisfactory to the Jews. Before long the Roman governor had to deal with a severe revolt.

Simon was assassinated in 135 B.C. After an interval during which his son-in-law attempted unsuccessfully to take his place, his son John Hyrcanus followed. He was at first backed by the Pharisees despite the fact that he was greatly influenced by Greek ideas, and this situation aggravated the rivalry between the two main political groups—the Pharisees and the Sadducees. After Hyrcanus' death in 104 B.C. the dissensions grew much worse and there was violence in the streets.

The position was not improved, and by about 65 B.C. Hyrcanus' grandsons, Aristobulus II and Hyrcanus II, were at war with each other for the control of Judea. The former had the support of the Sadducees, and the latter was backed by some of the Pharisees.

The famous Roman general Gnaeus Pompeius Magnus (Pompey) was, at this point, in the Middle East concluding his successful campaigns against a number of enemies of Rome. He was urged to go to Palestine to help resolve the civil war.

Aristobulus, who feared that Pompey would favour Hyrcanus, offered to surrender Jerusalem. His followers were not so ready to yield and began to prepare a resistance and to fortify Jerusalem. Pompey ordered a full scale siege of the city. In three months Jerusalem fell. Pompey captured it, and broke into the Temple. To his surprise he found the inner sanctum empty. It was, in fact, customary for the Jews to leave it so, as it was considered the exclusive preserve of God.

Pompey's capture of Jerusalem resulted in strict curbs on Judean independence. The Jews were reorganized into two states, Judea and Galilee, which were separated by a strip of land around Samaria. Hyrcanus was confirmed as High Priest of both states, but the title of prince was taken from him. He was, in effect, no more than the Roman governor, and he was placed humiliatingly under the supervision of the Roman governor of Syria.

> **The Pharisees and the Sadducees**
> *At about the time of Simon, there was a beginning of a party system in Jewish politics. Hitherto, Jews had either adhered to the old laws of Moses and the Torah, or they had favoured the ideas of their masters of the time, such as the Greeks or the Syrians. Now, Jewish political life became gradually coloured by a range of ideas supported by party groupings. The principal supporters of the old law drawn largely from the lower and middle classes, were called* Pharisees, *patriots who held that the Jews must remain separate from non-Jews of all kinds. Their main opponents were called* Sadducees *who represented largely the upper classes and supported the monarchy and the hereditary high priests, and interpreted the laws quite differently. They were also the more warlike party. Beyond these there were the judges, who were not allied to either, and the remaining adherents to the Maccabean cause.*

This picture shows a reconstruction of the entrance to Hyrcanus' fort built in Palestine in the second century B.C.

Herod the Great

Herod the Great was named King of Judea by the Roman Senate and invested in office in the Temple of Jupiter in Rome. His long reign (37-5 B.C.) was conducted in the grand fashion of Roman emperors.

THE Pompeian settlement did not work. The Romans used it as an excuse to extract vast new sums in taxation from a people already paying high taxes. Worse, Hyrcanus II, a weak man who was under the thumb of his Roman adviser, Antipater, allowed the taxation to continue. This sparked off a number of risings which seriously threatened the stability of the whole region. These risings occurred when Rome was involved in a life and death struggle between the forces of the old republic led by Pompey and those of progress led by Julius Caesar.

By 48 B.C. Caesar had defeated Pompey and started to round up his allies. Hyrcanus II, the High Priest, lent military support to Caesar. The great Roman responded by increasing Hyrcanus' power in Judea and even restoring some of the lands taken from him by the Pompeian settlement.

When Caesar was murdered in Rome in 44 B.C., the Jews who lived in the city and had been well treated by him regarded Rome's loss as their own.

In about 37 B.C. after a confused period of civil disorder, Herod, the son of Antipater, emerged as king of Judea with the sanction of Rome. Herod was

an extremely able man, cold, cruel, and cunning, but also cultivated and dignified. His first act was to arrange for the assassination of practically the entire Pharisee sanhedrin. Then he had Hyrcanus, whom he had deposed to get the throne, put to death. A few years later, Herod ordered his own wife's execution, followed by her mother's.

Imagine how the Jews reacted to this inglorious catalogue of crimes! Herod's record of crime, however, must not obscure the good that he did. Herod tried to ingratiate himself with his subjects by reconstructing the Temple in Jerusalem in the orthodox Jewish style of building. At the same time he erected or improved other buildings in the Greek and Roman style, which offended his people greatly. In Jerusalem he built a hippodrome, a stadium for gladiatorial shows and entertainments which were not favoured by the Jews.

Herod, however, was still a Jew himself, and he never forgot it. Although he suppressed the more democratic elements of the old Jewish constitution he ruled well and there was generally peace during the thirty-two years of his reign.

Sanhedrin
The sanhedrin was a kind of council of leading Jews who decided the vital matters concerning the Jewish people in Palestine, especially legal matters. It consisted of a number of priests, lawyers and scholars, and they elected a chairman, called the Nasi. The word sanhedrin came from the Greek meaning "sitting together", and this illustrates the influence of Greek democratic ideas on the Jews. The sanhedrin was really the highest council of state.

In the early days of the first century A.D. sanhedrins began to act as courts of law, sometimes to try religious offenders. Jesus of Nazareth was tried by a sanhedrin.

After the destruction of the Temple by Titus, the sanhedrin ceased to have political power and became a kind of advisory body on the interpretation of Jewish religion and law. Roman authorities sometimes recognized it as the proper body of Jews whom they consulted before making political or social decisions in Judea.

The Beginning of the End

A Time of Reformers

HEROD'S rule was not endured without resistance. He had tried hard to crush the influence of the Pharisees, the upholders of Jewish law, by encouraging the Sadducees, even choosing the members of the Sadducee sanhedrin. For a while the Pharisees were cowed, but sometime after 30 B.C. Hillel, who probably came from the Jewish community in Mesopotamia, was elected head of a new Pharisee sanhedrin. This was a signal event for the Jews.

Hillel, a man of magnetic personality, a very wise thinker, and personally courageous, soon dominated the Pharisee scholars. He unhesitatingly stated and restated the Jewish law, in a land which was under strict Roman jurisdiction. He became involved in endless arguments and discourses with Herod's administration, but he found time to codify Hebrew law, which had become a jumble of statutes. Hillel died, after Herod, in A.D. 10. He had not deflected the king from his chosen path, but he had inspired the Jews with a desire to achieve unity. What is more, Hillel's code became the basis of all future Jewish lawmaking.

Herod's death in 5 B.C. was followed by a general uprising of the Jews. The Romans took advantage of the disturbances and crushed the revolt mercilessly. Then they put Judea under direct rule of a procurator who inflicted heavy taxation upon the people. This resulted in further rebellion all over the land.

One of the rebel leaders was Judah of Galilee whose father Hezekiah had been put to death for treason. Judah led a band of well-organized guerillas

Hillel
The great Hillel (75 B.C.–A.D. 10) was chairman of the Pharisee sanhedrin during Herod's reign. To provide the Jews with an enduring code of laws, Hillel ruled that the written law (the Bible) was supreme and all other laws and customs must be based upon the scriptures.

Judah and his Zealot followers waged guerilla warfare against rich, Hellenized Jews. "We fight for our law [the Hebrew scripture]" was their motto.

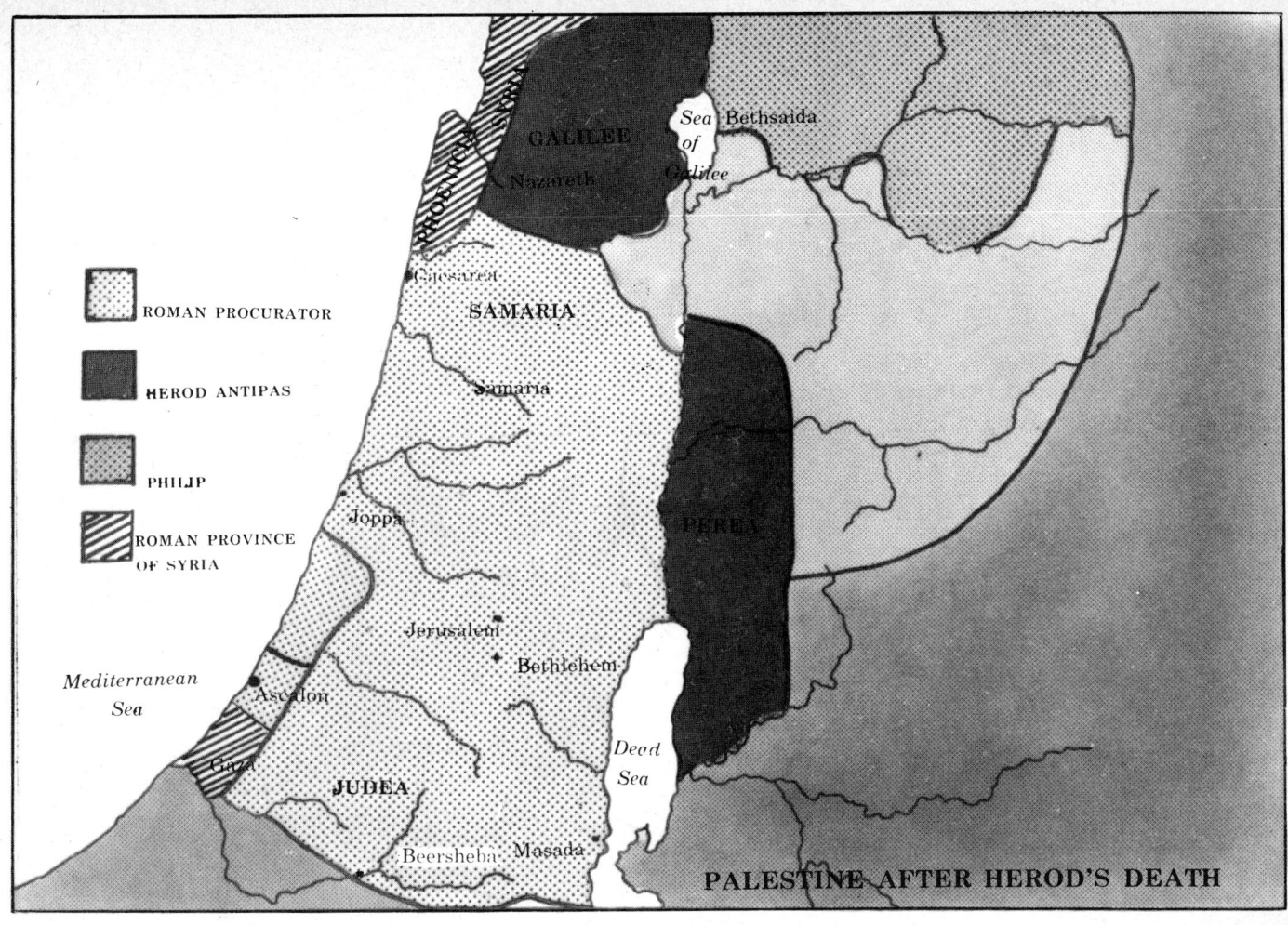

who attacked Roman officials and troops and also Jews who were on familiar terms with the Romans. Judah was caught and executed, but his followers carried on the struggle. They came to be known as the Zealots because they would not give up, and they remained outlaws for many years, constantly harassing officials and garrisons.

Palestine was rife with agitators and social and religious reformers at this time, who used such festivals as the Feast of the Passover and the Pentecost to organize demonstrations which often ended in bloodshed. But there were many peaceable reformers. Among them was a carpenter's son from Galilee named Joshua (Jesus). His followers called him the Messiah or Son of the Lord sent to deliver the Jews from foreign bondage, but his career was not regarded by the Jewish authorities as any more significant than those of other reformers of the time.

Upon Herod's death, Archelaus became ruler of Samaria, Judea and Idumea (an area at the southern end of Judea on the map). Archelaus' reign lasted until A.D. 6 when his territory was placed under a Roman procurator. Another of Herod's sons, Antipas, took over Galilee and Perea, and a third, Philip, was given the territory north-east of the Jordan River.

However, since there was general rebellion throughout these lands after Herod's death, the Emperor Augustus took advantage of the situation and in A.D. 6 took over the main territory of the Jewish homeland. Since Jerusalem was a notorious centre of discontent, the capital was removed to the city of Caesarea.

Jesus of Nazareth

JESUS of Nazareth was born a year or two after the death of Herod the Great. In his youth he discovered he had certain healing powers and in his spare hours he sometimes attempted to cure illnesses or infirmities. He also studied law, and became familiar with many Jewish writings, especially those of Hillel. In time, Jesus took to preaching, like many of the earlier prophets.

When he was about thirty, Jesus decided to give up his job and preach and heal as full-time occupations. Before long he acquired a following, and as it grew he found he had to organize the followers. So he picked a team of twelve friends who are known by Christians as his twelve disciples. These people managed the meetings, spread Jesus' teachings among the people and looked after his day to day needs.

Jesus gave many lectures. One of these was to a huge crowd assembled on the side of the Mount of Olives, just outside Jerusalem, which has become famous as the Sermon on the Mount. His message was simple and stated elementary rules of behaviour for men towards their fellow men, based on the brotherhood of man.

The Sadducees, who were at the time the ruling party in Palestine, objected to his teachings and they doubted his healing powers. So they summoned a sanhedrin and tried him before it for blasphemy. They had already got the agreement of the Roman governor, Pontius Pilate, who arranged for Jesus to be put to death.

At the time not many people thought much about Jesus' crucifixion, except of course his followers who considered him a martyr and called him the

"And when they had bound him, they led him away, and delivered him to Pontius Pilate the governor." (Matthew 27, verse 2)

Son of God, and the Messiah. And yet before long his teachings were being spread throughout the Roman world. In the fourth century, the religion which stemmed from Jesus' teachings, called Christianity, had become the official religion of the great Roman empire.

What brought this about? His ideas, his healing work, even the circumstances of his death, were not unusual for the time. But it is clear that he had an extraordinary power over his followers, one which continued after his death. His message continued to spread through Palestine. One man who at first regarded it as unacceptable and then suddenly became converted was a tent-maker from Tarsus called Saul. Better known to Christians as St. Paul, Saul gave the rest of his life to spreading the new faith. He became the most active worker that Christianity has ever had. In today's terms he would be regarded as having been the finest public relations man of all time.

Through his tireless campaigning for Christianity, his stream of letters and his lectures, Paul succeeded in carrying the message of Jesus as far as Greece, Egypt and Rome, and elsewhere, too. He made a great number of journeys throughout the Mediterranean area, most of which we know about, and the story of them and the talks he gave form a large part of the New Testament of the Christian Bible.

The main reason for the success of Paul's mission was that Christianity was a religion of comfort. It offered a happy and trouble-free life in the next world in return for proper behaviour in this world.

Once Christianity had reached Rome and other cities small groups of believers were formed and these grew into larger ones. More often than not Christians were persecuted by Roman emperors, for the faith was pronounced illegal. This did not stop its growth, but only drove it underground. Finally, in A.D. 325 Constantine, Emperor in the West who later became sole emperor of Rome, granted toleration to all Christians. Christianity is now one of the principal religions of the world.

Left: *Herod Agrippa, grandson of Herod the Great.*

Right: *In the historic gorge of Beth Horon, Jewish rebels routed Roman troops under General Gallus and brought the wrath of Rome down upon Jerusalem.*

Defeat for Rome

THE last and brief period of any happiness in the history of Judea began with the appointment, in A.D. 41, of Herod Agrippa, Herod the Great's grandson, as king of Judea. The country was granted self-government at the same time by the Roman emperor Claudius. Claudius also decreed that Jews throughout the Roman empire, which at the time stretched from Britain to the borders of Persia, were to be "permitted, uninterfered with, to observe the customs of their ancestors". It was the last time such toleration was extended to the Jews in Palestine.

Agrippa proved to be a sound and sympathetic ruler. He supported the Pharisees, joined the humblest folk in their religious devotions and festivals, and generally behaved like the kind

of leader the Jews had always welcomed most. But in so doing he offended the pro-Roman and more liberal Jewish classes, and they betrayed him to the Roman government. Agrippa died suddenly and mysteriously in A.D. 44 and Claudius, who may well have permitted Agrippa to be quietly disposed of, withdrew Judean independence. Once more, Roman procurators appeared, and the old conditions returned, bringing with them causes for revolt. It was the signal for further activity by the Zealots who had not, even during Agrippa's rule, disbanded completely.

In A.D. 64 a new procurator, Florus, was appointed, a man of greed and cruelty but little commonsense. He alienated the Jews by stealing a large quantity of gold from the Temple, the reconstruction of which had just been completed. The result was a serious riot. One impertinent Jew walked about the city with a cap begging for "Alms for Poor Florus", a sarcastic dig at the procurator. Florus retaliated with force, and hundreds of citizens were murdered, marking the beginning of general rebellion throughout the Jewish lands.

By A.D. 66 all Judea and Galilee were in revolt. It was not directed only at Roman overlords. Jews fought non-Jews in nearly every district of Palestine. It seemed to be as much a racial war as a general uprising of protest against years of ill-treatment. Cities like Samaria and Ascalon were sacked. The Roman authority in Jerusalem was overturned and a provisional government set up, elected by a general assembly of the citizens.

In Syria, the Roman general, Gallus, assembled an army and set out for Jerusalem to restore order. Because he did not have enough troops to carry out a siege of the fortified Jerusalem, Gallus decided to withdraw. A Jewish army trapped his army in the gorge of Beth Horon and killed 6,000 Roman troops. It was an unexpected and a humiliating defeat for Rome. The Romans decided, therefore, to bring the full weight of their military authority down upon the Jews.

The Fall of Jerusalem

THE Jewish victory encouraged a number of other peoples in the Middle East to join their cause. Bitter enemies for generations, the Samaritans buried their prejudices and came to Jerusalem offering help against the expected vengeance of Rome. The Idumeans and some volunteers from Mesopotamia also came to join the Jews. In the city, preparations were begun to withstand a prolonged siege, fortifications were strengthened, and fresh troops were recruited and trained.

The Romans, meanwhile, appointed a new commander for the area, Vespasian. Early in A.D. 67, he reached Antioch in Syria. He was joined by his son Titus, a handsome, dashing, bold soldier, with a legion collected from Egypt.

Vespasian advanced southwards and set up a post near the border of Galilee. The Jewish commander in Galilee was Joseph ben Mattathias, a descendant of the Maccabeans. He had recently been in Rome and was thought to know best how the Romans would conduct operations. Instead he surrendered the Galilean Jewish forces to Vespasian. This removed a serious danger to the Romans. Joseph then changed his name to Josephus Flavius and accompanied his new patron on the expedition to Jerusalem, which enabled him to write a detailed account of the campaign.

Vespasian marched down through Palestine, encountering less resistance than he expected. Early in A.D. 68 he occupied Jericho, and by the summer he was in control of the whole countryside except for Jerusalem and its immediate surroundings. At this point he heard of the death of the Emperor Nero and the seizure of power by one general after another.

In Jerusalem, meanwhile, the members of the

provisional government had quarrelled among themselves. Vespasian remained outside to let this disunity weaken their defences and so make his task much easier. But he was concerned about the seizures of power in Rome, and soon set out for Italy. On the way he heard that Rome now wanted him as emperor. He had left his son Titus behind with instructions to complete the conquest of Jerusalem.

The Jews had unfortunately not used the interval to resolve their differences or strengthen their position. Early in A.D. 70 Titus began to besiege the city. The defenders fought with magnificent heroism. Sometime in July the Temple itself was stormed and burned down, leaving standing only a section of the West Wall, which became to be known as the Wailing Wall. By September the city had fallen and resistance had collapsed.

In the spring of A.D. 70 the troops of Titus besieged Jerusalem. The Romans fought for the city street by street and house by house.

The Patriarchs

THE collapse of Jerusalem and the destruction of the Temple was not the complete end for the Jews. Judea and Galilee remained provinces in the Roman Empire and the populations were still largely Jewish. There were no more kings and no more high priests, but there were still leaders. The descendants of the great Hillel, in fact, dominated Palestine Jews. The first, after the fall of Jerusalem, was Gamaliel II, who was called the Nasi, or Patriarch. He was president of the sanhedrin. His position was handed down from him by hereditary succession for more than 300 years, and for most of that time the Nasi was looked upon by Romans as the spokesman of the Jewish people in Palestine.

After Jerusalem fell, hundreds and hundreds of Jews fled from Palestine. This was often called

Coins top row: *AE Sestertius, "Judaea Capta", struck in the reign of Vespasian (*A.D.* 69-79). Second row: Sestertius, "Judaea Capta", commemorating the victory of Titus, son of Vespasian, over Jerusalem (*A.D.* 79-81).*

Gamaliel and his pupils. For over three and a half centuries after Gamaliel's death, the recognized representative of the Jewish people was the Nasi, or president of the sanhedrin. Thus the political leadership of the Jews became unique in history—for it was conferred upon the scholar.

This is a copy of a drawing from the third century A.D., Mesopotamia, with the figure of the High Priest labelled Aaron. Aaron was the brother of Moses.

the "scattering" or "Diaspora", a word which describes collectively the dispersed Jews throughout the world. Some went to Mesopotamia, some to Parthia, some to Egypt, and some to Europe. In nearly every case they were still under Roman dominion, but more often than not they were tolerated and even given some measure of independence. They were allowed to follow their own way of life, to have their own laws—except where these clashed with Roman law—and to enjoy their own religion.

Meanwhile, Palestine was kept firmly under direct control, so sternly that revolts broke out. One, in A.D. 132 in the time of the emperor Hadrian, was a dangerous threat to stability in the Middle East. Led by Simon Bar Kozeba, known affectionately by his followers as Bar Kochba, or "Son of a Star", the rebels overcame large areas of Judea, drove the Roman government out of Jerusalem, and created a kind of independence that lasted for three years.

In 135 the emperor himself took command of the Roman forces, and put the revolt down at once, executing the leaders. Hadrian then decided that the Jews must be taught a lesson. Their law teachers were held to be the real instigators of revolt and so were put to death. Jerusalem was sacked and the population driven out. Many were enslaved and Judea was left desolate. Judaism was driven underground.

The situation did not improve with the passing of time. When Constantine I declared that Christianity was to be accepted throughout the Roman Empire, the status of the Jews deteriorated. There was a short respite in the reign of Julian the Apostate (361-63). An anti-Christian, he extended the hand of friendship to the Jews, corresponded with the Nasi, and even promised to rebuild the Temple. The opportunity was lost, however, on his death in 363 during a war with the Persians.

In 415, Gamaliel VI, the Patriarch, was expelled from office by the emperor Theodosius II, and the office was abolished.

The Diaspora

The Jews and Islam

In the fifth and sixth centuries A.D. Jews settled in many different lands, especially where Christianity was under attack. For example, a Jewish contingent of troops helped the Vandals in North Africa against forces of the Byzantines, and another assisted the Franks against Byzantines in Europe. This is not surprising, for Christian emperors in the West and East put many restrictions on Jews whom they regarded collectively as guilty of having murdered Jesus.

The Jews also found life easier in those lands of Europe where barbarians had driven out the Romans, such as Spain, northern Italy, what is now Yugoslavia, and France, making their living as travelling traders, businessmen, bankers, moneylenders, and technicians. Jewish traders and bankers had been operating in Europe for centuries, under varying degrees of restriction.

This meant that by the time of the collapse of the western Roman empire, towards the end of the fifth century A.D., the Jews were already becoming integrated into European society and were thus able to play an important part in the continent's future growth.

Throughout all this, the average Jew seldom neglected his religious duties, such as not working on the Sabbath, and invariably tried to live his life by those principles of the Torah which did not conflict with the laws of the society in which he resided.

In the seventh century a new religion, Islam, burst upon the Middle East and was soon carried

The Diaspora
Diaspora comes from a Greek word meaning "scattering". The Diaspora or scattering of the Jews from their homeland in Palestine dates very far back. By the third century, Jews were living in even the most distant provinces of the Roman Empire. By the time of the decline of the empire, Jews were thoroughly identified with European civilization, and in the fifth and sixth centuries they moved in large numbers to countries in the Middle East.

Typical Jewish costume under Islam, from about the eighth century. The yellow turban was worn by all Jewish men.

throughout the Mediterranean by armies of zealous believers. This religion was based upon the teachings of Mohammed, an Arabian merchant.

There were established communities of Jews in Arabia, and there had even been a kind of Jewish kingdom in the Yemen, where some Jews and Arabs had intermarried. So Mohammed was thoroughly familiar with the Jews, the Torah, and Jewish thinking. And he hoped very much to enlist the Jews' support in his new faith, which resembled Judaism: it recognized only one God, and revered the city of Jerusalem. Islam's doctrines incorporated in the holy book of Islam, the Koran, were similar to Judaism.

The enthusiasm of Mohammed's followers enabled him to form an army with which to carry the new ideas beyond the borders of Medina, and by his death he was master of Arabia.

The majority of the Jews declined to support Islam, and Mohammed responded by persecuting them. Following the rejection of Mohammed by the Jews, the Prophet downgraded Jerusalem and henceforth it was to Mecca that the faithful were to turn in prayer.

Mohammed's successors followed his policy, until they had overrun such vast areas that they found they could not afford to dispense with either the large number of Christians or Jews living there. So they moderated their policy towards non-believers, and from this time began the traditional spirit of toleration that has characterized Islam. There were restrictions, but these were not necessarily the same thing as persecution.

Khazars
The Khazars were an Asiatic people who occupied territory between the River Don and the River Volga in what is now the Ukraine (in Russia). They flourished from the eighth to the tenth century and were a powerful people for much of that time. Early in their history one of their rulers, Bulan, was converted to Judaism. His nobles and courtiers and many ordinary Khazars also converted, although they were not compelled to do so.

One of Bulan's descendant's, Obadiah, spread the religion by building synagogues and encouraging Jewish scholars from abroad to come to teach the Khazars.

The last king, Joseph, is believed to have corresponded with Hasdai (See page 48). The Khazars were finally overthrown and absorbed by the Russians.

The Jews in Moslem Spain

The Arab followers of Mohammed, who came to be known as Moslems, overran large areas of the Mediterranean coastline, including Syria, Egypt, and what is now Libya, Tunis and Morocco. In about 710 they crossed the Straits of Gibraltar, landed in Spain, and in a few years conquered the Visigoths scattered about the country. In their wake came many Jews—lawyers, teachers, craftsmen and peasant farmers.

The Jews who settled in Spain joined the small communities of their own people who had been there since Roman times. The Jews adopted Arab names, learned Arabic as well as Hebrew, and in general adjusted themselves to the Arab way of life. Their superior intelligence and culture marked them out for appointments to important positions in the country. Many Jewish professional people were employed directly by the Caliph, the Arab ruler of Spain.

One of the most interesting figures in this period was Hasdai ibn Shaprut (915-70), a doctor. Caliph Abdar Rahman III made him royal physician. Hasdai spoke Latin and several other languages, which made him useful as an interpreter as well. Soon, he was made foreign minister and before long he became the Caliph's principal adviser.

In this high position Hasdai never forgot his race or his people, and he watched over their interests in Spain, and elsewhere.

At the beginning of the eleventh century the Caliphate in Spain was overturned by an invasion of Berber people from North Africa, who were Moslem descendants of the Libyans of early Egyptian times. This broke up the Caliphate into small "kingdoms", for the Berbers were not highly organized people. Before long the Jews began to

Hasdai
Hasdai arranged for the translation of the medical works of the Greek biologist Dioscorides (first century A.D.) into Arabic. Dioscorides' work dominated medical thinking right up to the fifteenth century.

Talmud
The Talmud is a compilation of writings which incorporate the works of Jewish scholars and records of their discussions, especially about legal matters, over several centuries. There were two versions: the Jerusalem Talmud, which was completed in the fourth century A.D. and the Babylonian Talmud, completed in about 500. Both versions consist mainly of the Mishnah (the spoken law handed down from generation to generation since the time of Moses) and the Gemara (a commentary on the Mishnah).

All Jews study the Talmud in childhood, for it provides guidance on how to live a worthy life on this earth.

emerge as important people in these kingdoms.

Samuel ibn Nagrela (c.994-c.1063), a fine scholar, a poet and politician, became principal adviser to the emir, or "king", of Granada. In time Samuel came to rule Granada, in fact if not in name, for the emir preferred to spend his time in the pursuit of pleasure. All the emir asked for was a continual supply of money, and this Samuel provided.

Samuel was probably even more brilliant and versatile than Hasdai. He wrote an introduction to the Talmud which was a standard work for centuries. He wrote poetry celebrating victories he had won in the field of battle (for he was also a good military leader). He produced a dictionary of Hebrew. Above all, he patronized and encouraged learning on a wide scale and built up an extensive library which was admired by educated people everywhere in Europe.

When Samuel died he was succeeded by his son Joseph, a man of similar talents but whose overweening arrogance offended the whole community. Within three years he had been murdered, and all the Jews driven out of Granada.

A thirteenth century synagogue at Toledo in Spain. Jews first settled in Spain in Roman times. When the Arabs controlled Spain, Jews were prominent in many walks of life, but after Isabella the Catholic became Queen, the Inquisition (See page 60) made life almost impossible for practising Jews.

Jewish Philosophers of the Middle Ages

THE eleventh and twelfth centuries A.D. were a period of very bitter religious warfare and persecution throughout Europe and the Near East. Christian crusaders tramped along the roads of Europe or sailed across the Mediterranean Sea to Palestine which was in the hands of the Moslems and then of the barbarous Seljuk Turks. There they hoped to recover the Holy City of Jerusalem and make it free for Christian pilgrims from all over Europe to visit.

Both Arabs and Jews suffered during the Crusades, but out of these hard times Jewry emerged triumphant in the cultural and literary sense. It was already a matter of astonishment that the Jews had managed to keep alive their culture in lands foreign to them, where the environment was always different.

The Crusades
From the end of the eleventh century through the thirteenth century, the Crusades to the Holy Land continued. Although the major Crusades were begun to revenge Seljuk persecution of Christians, the Jews, as non-Christians, suffered great persecutions in the Crusade period. It was at this time that the Jews formulated a code of conduct, based on the Talmud, to see them through times of trial. The code provided that "when the enemy says 'deliver us one, we shall kill him and spare the rest,' rather that none be spared than surrender one." For centuries of persecution, the rule has stood as a testament to the dignity of the Jews.

The Jews produced a number of brilliant leaders in thought throughout the world in these centuries. Three of them were Solomon ibn Gabirol (1020-56), from Malaga in Spain, Judah ha Levi (1075-1141) from Toledo, and the greatest scholar of them all, Moses ben Maimon (Maimonides, 1135-1205) from Cordoba. These and many others preached and wrote for their people, encouraging them to be steadfast in their faith and principles, warning them of hard times and harsh persecutions that must come, stating and re-stating the law.

Judah ha Levi set out on a pilgrimage to Jerusalem calling on the way on as many Jewish communities as he could. He was enthusiastically welcomed by all of them. When he finally reached the outskirts of the Holy City he fell down and prayed. And as he lay prostrate, an Arab horseman accidentally trampled him to death.

Maimonides was thirteen when a new wave of Berber Moslems overran much of Spain and drove his family out of Cordoba. He spent the rest of his boyhood in Morocco where, although Jewish, he fell under the influence of Islam. Then he left for Egypt where there had been a Jewish community ever since early days. This community had enjoyed varying degrees of toleration, had sometimes been persecuted, and had also in Roman times had considerable privileges.

Maimonides studied medicine and, like Hasdai, was made court physician by the viceroy or vizier of Egypt. Maimonides held this post when Saladin seized power and made himself sultan of Egypt and Syria in 1174.

Maimonides became head of the Jewish community in Egypt. He was responsible for a large output of philosophical and legal writing. He produced a compendium of Jewish law in Hebrew. His influence was widespread—reaching far beyond the borders of Egypt, of Jewry even. He gathered round him a school of pupils and colleagues who, after his death carried his ideas further afield, and often suffered extreme misery and persecution for it.

One of Maimonides' works which caused the greatest trouble was a Guide of the Perplexed. *This was a restatement of Judaism on a completely reasonable basis. As a result, some of the ancient ideas and stories were modified and some were rejected. The guide was one of the great books of the Middle Ages, and Maimonides is held by the Jews as one of the most profound thinkers in their long history.*

The Hill of Darkness

Pope Urban II. After the Pope summoned Christendom to take steps to recover the Holy Land from the "Infidel", the Jews, as non-Christians, began to suffer greatly. From this time forward, Jewish writers called the town at which the Crusade was first preached not Clermont (which means the Hill of Light in French) but Har Ophel—the Hill of Darkness. (Mansell Collection)

Persecution Begins in Europe

AT the end of the eleventh century A.D. the Jews in Europe were subjected to a wave of persecution and maltreatment which was not unique in their history. Reports had been reaching Europe of unpleasant happenings to Christian pilgrims on visits to the Holy Land, Jerusalem and its surroundings. Shrines and other buildings associated with Christianity had been desecrated by the Moslem communities living there. Worse, Christian pilgrims to Jerusalem were beaten up, robbed, imprisoned, and even killed by the Seljuk Turks.

A meeting of leaders of the Christian church was held at Clermont in France in 1095. It was addressed by Pope Urban II, who summoned all Christian kings, princes, bishops, barons, knights and soldiers to form an international army with which to attack the Moslems and Turks in Palestine and recapture the Holy places. The event has since been called the First Crusade, and later there were to be several more crusades to the Holy Land.

How did this affect the Jews? It brought such a wave of misery for them in all quarters of Europe that Jewish historians referred to the Clermont meeting as the meeting on the Hill of Darkness (the town is on a hill).

Almost immediately Christians began to form gangs and rushed about the countryside in search of Jews to maim or murder. That they should visit the sins of the Moslems on the Jews, who were themselves often opposed to the Moslems, seems very unreasonable. There had, of course, been hostility between Christians and Jews ever since Roman days, but they accepted the same Ten Commandments, one of which was "Thou shalt not kill". The Crusaders, however, believed that it was their duty to suppress all those who did not accept Christianity, and thus organized a reign of terror against all Jews. Here and there local authorities intervened to save some Jews, but they could only reduce the terror a little.

The persecutions went on in Europe over the next four centuries. The Jews conducted themselves during these times with courage and honour. There were exceptions, but on the whole they declined to accept the alternative to death or torture which was abandonment of their faith and acceptance of Christian baptism. The Christian mobs hardly improved the image of their faith by the savage manner in which they brawled in the streets, wielding all manner of weapons, and hurling every kind of insult. Indeed, their behaviour served only to make the Jews stick together much more closely and to display a dignity that grew in stature as the persecutions became more ferocious.

Left: *A synagogue at Worms in Germany, first built in 1035. Although there had been preliminary outbreaks of violence against the Jews after the Clermont meeting, on Sunday, May 18, 1096, the first organized attack of Christian savagery occurred at Worms: more than 700 people lost their lives.*

The Jews in England

WHEN William, Duke of Normandy, conquered England in 1066, he set out to change the whole structure of English society. Many Jews who had been living in a Jewish community of long standing in Normandy took advantage of these changes and came to England to settle. By the end of the century there were Jews in many English cities, notably London, York, Winchester, Lincoln, Bristol and Norwich.

The persecution which followed the launching of the First Crusade did not at first affect the Jews in England. The Norman kings evidently regarded them as valuable members of society, and indeed Jews under duress elsewhere in Europe could expect to find refuge in England.

The situation changed, however, after the death of Henry I in 1135, when the country endured nineteen years of civil war between Henry's daughter Matilda and her cousin Stephen. Partly as a result of general discontent and misery over the unstable condition of the country, especially its economy, people turned on the Jews who seemed in many ways to be better off.

On Easter Eve in 1144, for example, a young apprentice called William, who lived in Norwich, was found dead in a wood. The story was put about that some Jews had killed him to provide a victim with which to celebrate their Passover feast. It is amazing that although the boy was found unwounded (he had clearly died from a fit), many people accepted this version. It sparked off a whole series of "Jew-hunts". Soon, the Jews were blamed for all manner of disasters, natural and otherwise.

At the same time the Christians accepted money from rich Jews to help build cathedrals and monasteries. One Jewish banker, Aaron of Lincoln, is said to have provided the funds, on loan and at interest

Opposite: *Caricature of English Jews is dated 1233. In the thirteenth century Jews were very heavily taxed by the crown. The drawing shows Isaac of Norwich, the richest Jew of his time, wearing the crown of Henry III to show that he was the king's property. (Crown Copyright.)*

Below: *The picture of two English Jews is from a manuscript dated about 1275. They wear a badge—the tablets of Moses—on their robes. (British Museum.)*

rates, to erect nearly a dozen monasteries and both Lincoln and Peterborough cathedrals.

During the coronation of Richard I at Westminster in 1189, an attack was made on the Jewish community in London, and many people were murdered. Other towns then followed suit, and the worst tragedy occurred at York. There, the Jews were driven out of their own living area and took refuge in the castle. It was besieged, and when they realized that they could no longer hold out, they declined to surrender. Instead, they killed all their wives and children and then slew each other.

In the thirteenth century, official policy in England was heavily against the Jews. It was chiefly demonstrated in the special taxes the Jews had to pay. So much had to be paid that in 1254 the Jewish leader Elias begged the king to be allowed to leave the country with his people. Henry III responded by forbidding them to leave. Then he seized the remnants of their property and distributed it among the members of his family, including his eldest son Edward I who expelled the Jews altogether from England and Wales in 1290.

Jewish Costume
A distinct form of dress is traditionally based upon the Biblical instruction to the Hebrews: "After the doings of the land of Egypt, wherein ye dwelt, ye shall not do..." That Jews should dress differently from non-Jews was stated clearly in a sixteenth century rabbinical code: "No child of the Covenant shall dress after the manner of Gentiles nor wear sleeves."

While this was the Jews' own choice, dress regulations were issued and enforced by the Christian church and many civil authorities in the Middle Ages.

The most distinctive feature of Jewish costume was the pointed hat—it was worn with pride and was as easily recognized a symbol of Jewry in Medieval times as is the six-pointed Star of David (Magen David) in modern times.

The badge, however, was bitterly resented by the Jews. It was first introduced into England in 1218, in Castile (Spain) in 1219, in Provence (France) in 1234 and in the Papal States in 1257. The badge was usually in the shape of a ring or circle, and the colour was usually yellow.

In England, however, the badge was first a piece of white cloth shaped to resemble the Tablets of Moses, later changed to yellow. In France it was a red and white circular piece of cloth.

The First Expulsions

THE Jews fared no better in France or in Germany than they had in England. As soon as the First Crusade was launched in 1096 the French authorities turned on the Jewish communities and forced them to choose one of two alternatives: renouncement of Judaism and acceptance of Christianity or persecution and loss of civil rights. Few Jews were willing to give up their faith so they suffered.

In many places there were riots which resulted in the deaths of Jews, often in large numbers. At Worms three hundred and fifty were killed in one outbreak, and as many at Prague, the capital of Bohemia. The Crusaders, who captured Jerusalem, murdered almost all the Jews living there in 1099.

The attacks went on throughout the twelfth century. What happened in England was repeated in France and Germany. Then in 1215 the Pope, Innocent III, opened a Church Council and introduced a series of edicts, some of which were directed against Jews. These edicts received almost universal support. They included: excusing any Crusaders from paying interest on loans obtained from Jews; barring Jews from holding State office; the payment of taxes to the Church for lands owned by Jews; the wearing of clothing to distinguish Jews from Christians.

 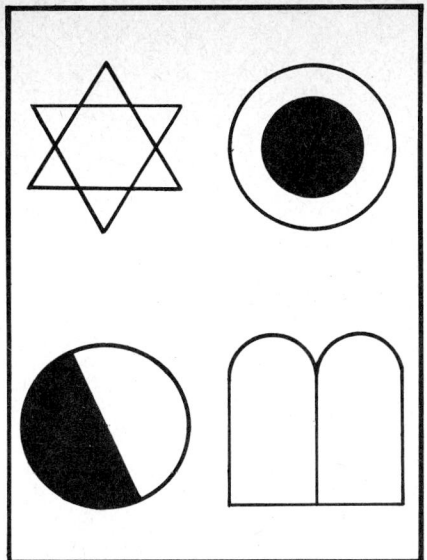

The four pictures show various forms of Jewish costume, and the badges Jews were required to wear. From left to right: a 14th-century French costume, 13th-century German costume (depicting Süsskind of Trimberg, a Jewish troubadour), a 14th-century Spanish Jewess, and three different kinds of badges and the Star of David.

Once the edicts were published, persecution of Jews gathered momentum. Eventually it led to total expulsion from several countries.

The first major expulsion was from England and Wales. In 1253 Henry III decreed that no Jews should be allowed to stay in England except as servants of the king. In 1290 Edward I decided that they must leave altogether. They were given three months to go, during which time they were guaranteed protection from violence. It was an empty promise for on one occasion a whole shipload of Jews was pushed out into the Thames without a helmsman.

In France the situation was as bad, if not worse. The Jews were first expelled in 1182 by the king, Philip Augustus. Succeeding kings continued to persecute them, and in 1306 almost all Jews were arrested and exiled. Their property was confiscated and they had only four weeks to get out.

In Germany there were no royal expulsion orders, but individual persecutions were deliberately overlooked, and in some cases encouraged. In 1298 an entire community at Nuremberg was butchered. In 1337 the city council of Deckendorf authorized the citizens to murder the Jewish community. When the Black Death swept through Europe in 1348-49 (this plague more than halved the population of Europe) the Jews were generally blamed.

Toleration in Poland

By the twelfth century Poland had become a nation chiefly of Slav people with a sizeable community of Jews. In the 1240's Russian invaders overran Poland and crippled its trade and industry. Then they withdrew, leaving the Poles to reconstruct their battered nation. This coincided with widespread persecutions of Jews in France and Germany, so the Polish kings welcomed immigrant Jews. King Boleslav granted them the special protection of the government by means of a charter in 1265. Poland was not long in reaping the benefit of its generous attitude to the Jews. Immigrants opened up new commercial enterprises and provided funds for building and other services.

Unfortunately, the fear created by the Black Death spread to Poland and for a while Jews suffered persecution and killing. But a century later, the king, Casimir the Great, tried to redress the earlier wrongs and continued the policy of toleration. Jews were allowed to reside anywhere. Court cases which involved them were referred to the king himself for decision.

The toleration resulted in a flourishing of Jewish culture and a rich period of business activity that benefited the whole nation. The country almost seemed to be a new home for Jews. Later kings extended privileges to them, allowing them a kind of independence in which they could have their own judges. The Jews were even permitted to have a Chief Rabbi.

Twelfth to thirteenth century typical costume—from Poland.

The celebration of the Passover feast. A drawing of Spanish Jews in the fourteenth century.

Mezuzah
A mezuzah (mezuzah is the Hebrew word for doorpost) is a scroll of parchment on which are written some verses from the Book of Deuteronomy. These verses are an exhortation to obedience. The scroll is put in a container and fixed on the upper right door post of a house or room. Some mezuzahs were decorated with pictures around the text. Mezuzahs were meant to remind Jews that all their possessions were gifts of God. (Mezuzah above is in the Jewish Museum, London.)

Defence of the Faith

WE have seen the way in which the Jews flourished for a time in Spain, how they dominated everyday life, even the government, when the country was in the hands of the Moslems. As the Christians gradually encroached upon the land, however, the influence of the Jews diminished, and they began to endure the kind of existence their fellow Jews were suffering in England and elsewhere.

In the ninth century a scheme had been introduced by the Byzantine Christians whereby Jews could defend their faith in public debate. They were offered money to desert the cause of Judaism but not many yielded to the temptation.

The exercise was repeated in later generations in Europe, particularly in Spain where it became more of a public examination by the authorities than a free discussion. Some of the leading Jewish scholars in Spain were summoned to such debates and many of them defended Judaism with great skill.

One rabbi, Moses Nachmanides (1194-1270) was ordered to a debate before the king of Aragon (one of the northern kingdoms of Spain) and he conducted his defence so well that the judges almost decided in his favour. But of course they could not actually do so, for it would admit that Judaism was a better religion than Christianity. Nachmanides published his arguments and circulated copies widely. The king ordered the rabbi's expulsion from Spain. Nachmanides was not the only rabbi expelled from Spain, but he was regarded as a particularly dangerous influence.

Spain—Inquisition and Expulsion

THE Jews had proved almost indispensable to the Moslems in Spain. They were every bit as useful to the first Christians. They proved their worth in battle, and Alfonso VIII of Castile conferred knighthood on some of their captains, even though knighthood was essentially a Christian honour. Pedro the Cruel, king of Castile (1350-69), favoured the Jews. One of them, Samuel Abulafia, reached the high rank of Treasurer to the Crown. But Pedro was the last Spanish king to treat the Jews well. When he was deposed in 1369 his successor made the Jews pay for his favour. They were forced to wear the yellow badge as a sign of shame. Any non-Jew seeing the badge would jeer at the wearer, perhaps throw stones at him, possibly even beat him up.

In 1391, a severe anti-Jewish riot broke out in Seville. Thousands of Jews were killed. This sparked off riots elsewhere. In Toledo hundreds of Jews were massacred. In Barcelona the whole Jewish community was exterminated. The only major settlement to survive was in Granada, a small kingdom still ruled by Moslems.

1391 was a black year for the Jews, not only because nearly 100,000 of them perished in the riots, but also because, for the first time in their history, many Jews gave way under the strain of persecution, and accepted baptism as Christians, to save themselves from further misery. One convert actually became Bishop of Burgos.

The unfortunate converts did not reap much benefit. They were referred to as "Marranos", the Spanish word for pigs, and were insulted or avoided in the streets. It took a generation for the name Marrano to be accepted at all. Meanwhile, those Jews who had not given way were subjected to fresh waves of restriction and insult. They were banned from entering any profession; they were made to

Auto-da-fé
When the Inquisition had conducted a series of trials of suspects, a ceremony was then held in public in which judgment was pronounced. This was called an auto-da-fé, *which is Spanish for act of faith, because the guilty were expected to beg forgiveness and ask to be accepted into the Christian faith before they were punished.*

The condemned people, usually though not always Jewish or of Jewish descent, were sentenced and handed to the government authorities for punishment. Prayers were then read for the souls of the victims.

live in a community cut off from the rest of society; their trading activities were curbed; they could not carry arms.

The new generation of Marranos, however, paid lip service to the forms of Christianity but were still Jewish at heart. After all, the beliefs and way of life of three thousand years' standing cannot be erased in one, two or even three generations. By their pretence the Marranos succeeded in recovering many high positions formerly held by the Jews in Spanish society. They intermarried with the Christian nobility and gentry. They entered the law, the army, the civil service, even the Church.

In 1474 Isabella the Catholic became queen of Castile. She married Ferdinand of Aragon, thereby joining nearly all Spain into one kingdom. Together they set out to eradicate heresy, that is, belief in any doctrine that differed from the Catholic Christian church. Heresy was not necessarily "unbelief"; it meant rather "misunderstanding" or "misinterpretation". Although there were a number of kinds of heresy, clearly the purge was directed against the secret Jews—the Marranos.

The king and queen employed the Inquisition, a tribunal of officials of the Catholic Church to carry out the purge.

Thousands of Marranos, many hiding or at all events disguising their beliefs, were detected and handed to the Inquisition for punishment, which meant either death, or life sentence as galley slaves in Spanish ships. This did not satisfy the king and queen. By royal decree of 1492, all professing Jews were given four months to leave the country altogether. The number of exiles is said to have been nearly 200,000 and they suffered terrible hardships.

To generate support for the Inquisition, Christian artists sometimes drew pictures of Jews desecrating churches—although there was no factual evidence of such "crimes".

Pope Paul IV, the Founder of the Ghetto.

This drawing resembles a woodcut from an old Jewish book from Prague, Czechoslovakia, of a ghetto.

The Ghettos

FROM the earliest days of Jewish emigration to Europe and elsewhere the Jews had tended to live together in communities. Often they found life easier if they stayed together. The process had at first been voluntary. But after 1180 an edict from Rome stated that Christians and Jews must not live together. For many years this was treated fairly widely with contempt in cities where tolerance existed, especially in Italy.

The republic of Venice which was a smallish nation of traders and sea-farers who had a large majority of the Mediterranean trade, feared the competitiveness of the Jewish traders and bankers who, having been driven out of Spain and elsewhere, now found some sort of refuge in Italy. In 1516 a decree was made ordering all resident Jews in Venice to be moved into one quarter of the city which was walled off. It was known as the Ghetto Nuovo (New Foundry) and the word ghetto came to mean the quarter of any city in which Jews were segregated.

The ghetto in Venice was not the first, but its story provides a picture of what it was like to be a Jew living in a ghetto. Everything appeared to be geared to making one feel different, outcast, unwanted, and finally less than human. The gateway was a low one, with thick doors, which locked from the inside only. The doors were guarded day and night by Christian soldiers. No Jew was allowed out, nor any Christian let in after dusk. Offences against this rule were severely punished.

Ghettos were sometimes only one street sealed off at each end, and sometimes a network of streets surrounded by walls. Although by the laws of nature the community increased in population the land area did not. So the Jews had to build upwards, adding storeys to existing buildings, which were

sometimes not sound and collapsed or caught fire.

Being compelled to live in a ghetto was not the only indignity suffered by Jews at this time. The yellow badge had to be worn. A host of petty taxes and regulations were imposed. They might have to pay to get into public buildings or public places. They could not ride in any form of conveyance, nor could they employ Christian servants or labourers. They were not allowed to own a copy of the Talmud. They were not allowed to trade in any kind of new goods.

On the other hand, despite the restrictions of the ghetto the Jews maintained their religion, cultivated their laws to adapt to their new circumstances, and kept their schools going. A child in the ghetto might be short of food, but his education was never neglected.

All the same, the system was bound to have a degenerating effect on all but the strongest, for physical conditions must often have been intolerable.

Yiddish and Ladino
Yiddish is a language spoken by Jews of mainly European origin, with a strong emphasis on German. It arose among German Jews who in the thirteen and fourteen centuries emigrated to Eastern Europe. It was a mixture of German, Hebrew and Polish, Greek and Russian. Another language spoken by Jews is Ladino. This is the language of the Spanish Jews of the Middle Ages, and it also has words from other languages, like Greek and Turkish. Ladino is still spoken in Israel and in some parts of the Eastern Mediterranean.

The Dawn of Liberty

The Jews Go to the East

THE unfortunate Spanish exiles sold their properties at great loss and they were not allowed to take their valuables with them. On the journeys from Spain they endured disease, highway robbery and murder. Some went by land to other countries in Europe where in many cases they had to hide from the authorities. In some cities in Italy starving Jews were offered food by monks in return for becoming Christians. Some of the Jews went across the Straits of Gibraltar into North Africa. Many of them, however, managed to get to the Near East where, since the fall of Constantinople in 1453, the Ottoman Turks were masters of a huge empire which included Syria, Palestine, Mesopotamia and Asia Minor. There they were welcomed by the Sultan Bayazid II who exclaimed when he heard of the Spanish expulsion: "Do you call this king (Ferdinand) the Wise One, when he depopulates his own dominions in order to enrich mine?"

New communities of Jews sprang up all over the Ottoman empire. They were joined by quite a number of Marranos who seized the opportunity of reverting to their true faith in peace. And they more than repaid the Sultan for his kindness by bringing their talents and skills into the service of the empire. Doctors, lawyers, teachers, craftsmen, bankers, all were busily employed. Jewish printers brought printing equipment and set up the first press at Constantinople. Jewish immigrants managed shipping agencies, textile factories and banks, and they also entered politics in much the same way as their ancestors had done in Spain hundreds of years before.

The career of one Spanish Jew was especially

Beatrice de Luna, the aunt of Joseph Nasi, became known as Gracia Nasi after the family moved to Constantinople. She was the most beautiful and most adored Jewess of her day. Gracia Nasi had married the head of the Mendes firm, a large banking empire.

Ashkenazim— Sephardim
When the Jews wandered through Europe in the Middle Ages and settled in various countries, they came to be described collectively with a different name in each country. Later, European Jews were described by one or the other of two names. The Ashkenazim were German or Jews of German-descent, including those who went to Eastern Europe. The Sephardim were the Spanish Jews, and this term also applied to those who, after expulsion from Spain, settled in the East Mediterranean.

Today, these terms are not easy to define. There are language pronunciation differences between Ashkenazim and Sephardim, and there are also differences in religious ceremonial. Of the world's twelve million or so Jews, three-quarters are Ashkenazim.

interesting. João Miguez' family was driven out of Spain in 1492. They went to Portugal where conditions were not much better, and after a series of adventures he and his aunt, the rich Beatrice de Luna Mendes, reached Constantinople. She had a beautiful daughter, Reyna, whom João married, and they then assumed the old Jewish family name of Nasi.

Joseph Nasi was a man of the highest intellect, subtlety and versatility. He was also rich and soon came to the notice of the sultan, Suleiman the Magnificent, who gave him an important post in government.

Nasi became very influential at court, and his services as diplomat and political adviser were well rewarded by lands in Syria given him by the sultan. When Suleiman died, his successor Selim II retained Nasi's services, made him Duke of Naxos and gave him a number of beautiful islands in the Aegean Sea. Nasi is said to have influenced the king of Poland to increase toleration for the Jews there. He is also said to have considered setting up a new nation for Jews from Europe on an island not far from Venice.

Selim's successor, Murad, forced Nasi to retire. He had become alarmed at his enormous powers, but he did not persecute him, nor did he restrict other Jews. Many others reached high positions and the early days of the Ottoman Empire were greatly enriched by the presence of Jewish communities.

The Court of Suleiman the Magnificent, where Joseph Nasi, Duke of Naxos, was adviser. When Nasi arrived in Turkey he brought with him five hundred Jews—all the people who had served the rich Mendes banking empire in Venice.

Marranos and the Age of Discovery

THE sixteenth century for the Jews was a period of contrast. In the Ottoman empire they had every opportunity for flourishing. In Poland they were welcomed. But in France, Spain, Germany and Italy they were not wanted. It was a century of tremendous intellectual and artistic achievement for Christians in Western Europe, part of the age called the Renaissance, when painters, sculptors, architects and poets produced many of the greatest works of art of all time in their respective fields, almost entirely without the help of the Jews.

The century also witnessed the opening up of what was called the New World (North and South America) and the exploitation of the sea route to India and the Far East. This Age of Discovery was something in which the Jews could and did share. It was a Jew, Abraham Zacuto, the leading astronomer in Spain and Portugal in the second half of the fifteenth century, who actually provided the astrolabes for the epoch-making voyage of Vasco da Gama around the Cape of Good Hope to India in 1497-9.

Jewish money financed many expeditions of the time; one was that of Columbus. Christopher Columbus, who by landing in Cuba in 1492 thought he had discovered the westward route to China and India but in fact had discovered the Americas, had been largely financed by Marranos (Spanish and Portuguese Jews who had accepted Christianity although many still practised Judaism privately). A loan was put up by two Marrano bankers, Santagel and Sanchez, and much of the organization and provisioning was carried out by Marranos. When Columbus drafted his report on the voyage for the king and queen of Spain his preface included the words: "And thus, having expelled all the Jews from all your kingdoms and dominions, in the same

Below: *a Jewish wedding feast from the time of Columbus and the voyages of discovery.*

Jewish brides often wore wedding rings beautifully carved with a replica of the Temple at Jerusalem.

month . . . Your Highnesses commanded me that, with a sufficient fleet, I should go to the said parts of India . . . " He is not recorded as having taken any Jews with him, but it is possible, for Columbus was of Jewish descent himself.

The Portuguese voyages to India and the Far East and to Brazil and other parts of South America were similarly funded with Jewish money and helped with Jewish scientific skill.

In the sixteenth century many Jews made their way to the Spanish Netherlands (what is now Belgium). At Antwerp, the most important port, Jews found refuge, although they were not popular. When the Dutch won their independence from Spain at the end of the century, Amsterdam in Holland became the principal port of the Low Countries and there the Jews were able to found a community in comparative peace.

There is a famous legend about the first Jewish community in Amsterdam. A brother and sister, Manuel Pereira and Maria Nunez, left Portugal among a group of Marranos seeking refuge. The ship was captured by the English and brought to port. An English knight fell in love with Maria Nunez, who was extremely beautiful, and wanted to marry her, but Queen Elizabeth I insisted on seeing the girl first. The queen was immediately impressed by Maria's looks and manners, and forthwith liberated all the Marranos on the ship. Maria, however, did not wish to marry the knight, and begged to be allowed to go to Amsterdam with her brother and the rest of the emigrants. The queen consented, and a few years later in 1598, Maria and her brother, safely established in Amsterdam, were joined by her mother and several other relations. Maria then fell in love with another emigrant and they were married. It was said to be the first Jewish wedding ceremony and feast held in Amsterdam.

Holland Helps the Jews

ALTHOUGH in the sixteenth century the Jews in Antwerp had endured less hardship and restriction, the king of Spain, Charles V, who was also Emperor of the Holy Roman Empire decided to expel them from the city in 1550. This time the Jews did not have to look far for refuge. The French king, Henry II, had for some time been encouraging the Jews to come to France and now admitted anyone who wished to come in. Henry gave them guarantees of rights, and some other countries soon followed suit. Jews were also welcomed in Holland, especially in the city of Amsterdam, and early in the seventeenth century the king of Denmark welcomed them.

The Dutch had grounds for being particularly grateful to the Jews. Holland was beginning to challenge the mastery of the seas and the monopoly of trade in the East and the West held by Spain and Portugal. To some extent this was due to the skilful trading activities of Marrano bankers and merchants. Amsterdam Jewish financiers invested large sums in the Dutch West India Company which was exploiting riches in the Americas. When the Dutch decided to fight for the large area of Brazil in about 1624, which was then under the dominion of Portugal, Jews not only provided funds for the expedition, but also supplied many young men at arms. It was a successful expedition.

Many Dutch Jews went to the colonies in Cuba, Mexico and on the east coast of what is now the United States. After the Portuguese succeeded in winning Brazil back from the Dutch in about 1654, a fresh wave of Marranos had to find new homes. They came to North America and landed at New Amsterdam, one of the first Dutch settlements. The Governor of New Netherlands, Peter Stuyvesant, was unwilling to accept the Jews, but his employers, the Dutch West India Company, many of whose

Zacutus Lusitanus (1576-1642) was a leading Marrano doctor, who in 1625 was expelled from Portugal. He fled to Amsterdam and later became famous for his medical writings.

investors were Jews, reversed the Governor's decision. Incensed by his intolerance, they applied pressure on the company in Amsterdam. They drew up a letter of protest at Stuyvesant's conduct, and suggested that if the Marranos were not admitted they would almost certainly go to the French settlements in North America and take all their money and expertise with them. The company saw the light.

The man responsible for the pressure was a Marrano scholar called Menasseh ben Israel (1604-57). His father had been a Marrano exile from Portugal, and Menasseh had been given an excellent education. Even at a young age Menasseh became a leading figure among the Amsterdam Jews, for he could speak nine languages, he was thoroughly versed in the Talmud and all other important Jewish writings, and he had cultivated an atmosphere of the mysterious about his faith. He believed that Jews could not be reassembled together as a race until they had been readmitted into Britain. The Puritans in England were receptive to his ideas because they regarded themselves as the lost tribes of Israel. They favoured the Jews and pressed Oliver Cromwell, Lord Protector of England, Scotland and Ireland, to admit them into the country.

Cromwell invited Menasseh to London for talks, and in 1655, at a large meeting of lawyers, religious experts and government officials the idea was thrashed out. While the lawyers saw no obstacles to admitting the Jews, the politicians, probably influenced before the meeting, said that the Jews would undermine the business community and take over many financial concerns. The talks broke down, but a good point—the legal one— had been made in favour of the Jews.

Menasseh and his colleagues still hoped, however, that Cromwell would let the Jews into England. As it was, Cromwell made no official declaration that they might come, but he admitted them unofficially. Cromwell's tolerant attitude paved the way for their more regular acceptance in the reign of Charles II (1660-85.)

Menasseh ben Israel, a friend of the famous Dutch painter Rembrandt, was one of the most powerful of Amsterdam Jews. A master of nine languages, ben Israel petitioned Cromwell to admit Jews into England because he believed that the Jews would not return to Zion until they had first been dispersed throughout the world.

Bar Mitzvah
When a Jewish boy reaches the age of thirteen he is regarded as old enough to understand the Jewish religion and to observe the basic teachings of Moses. He is formally confirmed in the religion by means of a ceremony called the Bar Mitzvah. At this he has to demonstrate his knowledge of the Torah and what it means. At one time he would have had to prepare and deliver a lecture on the subject.

A rabbi blowing the shofar in a synagogue. The shofar was the ancient ram's horn trumpet of the Hebrews calling the faithful to prayer.

Yom Kippur
From sunset on Friday until nightfall on Saturday, every week, Jews have a day of rest, or a sabbath. This commemorates the fact that God created the earth in six days and rested on the seventh.

One very important sabbath is the Day of Atonement, which is called Yom Kippur. On this day Jews are supposed to cleanse themselves of sin by confession, and they do no work, eat no food and have nothing to drink. Yom Kippur is one of the oldest of the Jewish customs, and it is believed to have stemmed from the day when Moses descended from Mount Sinai with the sacred tablets of the Ten Commandments.

A Famous Philosopher

SEVENTEENTH century Europe produced a number of great thinkers and philosophers, like Francis Bacon Rene Descartes and Isaac Newton. One of the foremost was Baruch (or Benedict) de Spinoza, who was born in Amsterdam in 1632 of Marrano parents.

This remarkable man, after a sound education, earned a meagre living as a telescope lens grinder. It was a dull enough job, and during his leisure hours he studied the philosophical writings of all the leading thinkers of the previous two thousand years, from Plato, Aristotle, and Lucretius onwards. He was also particularly interested in the work of the French philosopher Descartes (1596-1650), whose ideas were based on one of his own sayings, "I think, therefore, I am." From this saying Descartes deduced the idea that "an infinite perfect being (namely, God) exists in my mind; as I am myself finite, this idea must have been implanted there by an infinite being, who must therefore exist." It was a simple way of proving the existence of God and it was the sort of argument which someone who was familiar with Jewish law and thinking could find sympathetic. Spinoza set out to develop it even further than Descartes.

By the age of twenty-four, although he had not as yet published any works, Spinoza had become extremely well known through his lectures. The Jewish elders in Amsterdam, however, disapproved sternly of his teachings, and were even more put out by the fact that Spinoza refused to conform to Jewish customs. He was not prepared to change his ways, so the rabbis expelled him from the faith.

Baruch (Benedict de) Spinoza (1632-77) was excommunicated by the Jewish authorities when he was only twenty-four. One of the great philosophers, Spinoza's view of Jewish history and law clashed with that of the Amsterdam elders.

Possibly he had not helped himself by rejecting many of the principles of Maimonides, regarded as Judaism's greatest thinker of the Middle Ages.

One field in which Spinoza disagreed with orthodox Jewish thought was in that of law. The orthodox view was that "law derives from authority, that authority ceases when its ability to enforce obedience ceases". Spinoza also stated that freedom to think as he chooses is every man's right, but his actions are rightly subordinate to the state or to the ruler who may define faith.

Spinoza felt, too, that Jesus of Nazareth and his teachings were more important than Moses and Mosaic law, and he recommended Jews to study the New Testament, which is essentially the Christian part of the Bible.

It is not surprising that Spinoza found himself in trouble with his fellow Jews; nor were his advanced views acceptable to Christians. He was offered a post as professor of philosophy at Heidelberg university in Germany, a country which did not as a rule give many opportunities to Jews in any walk of life. Spinoza declined on the grounds that he might have to surrender complete independence of thinking. He died in 1677.

The exterior of the Marranos' synagogue, built in Amsterdam in the seventeenth century. It was one of the finest buildings in the city.

Left: *"Jew" Suss and* right: *Moses Mendelssohn.*

The Burden Begins to be Lifted

WE have seen that for a long time Poland was the one European country which welcomed the Jews. Now in the period 1618-48 nearly all Europe was involved in a bitter struggle between the Catholic and Protestant powers, known as the Thirty Years War. When it was finally over Europe was exhausted.

The Cossack people in the Ukraine, a province southwest of Russia then under Polish dominion, chose this moment to rise in revolt. They objected not only to being governed by the Poles, but also to the fact that many agents of Polish land owners were Jewish. They set upon and murdered their masters in great numbers. Many Poles, to their shame, betrayed Jews to the Cossacks in the hope of saving their own skins. This was followed by attacks on the Jewish communities in Poland itself.

A few years later the Czar of Russia, who had been looking for an excuse to attack Poland, decided to come in on the side of the Cossacks and invaded. In their path of conquest through Poland, the Russians murdered or expelled whole communities of Jews. Over a ten year period some 250,000 Jews perished. The survivors began to leave the country and flee to many different places—Constantinople, Venice, Budapest, Vienna and Amsterdam—where they sought refuge in the ghettos or among the established communities. It

The execution of "Jew" Suss.

The Execution of "Jew" Suss
Joseph Ben Issacher Suskind Oppenheimer (1697-1738) was a German Jewish financier who reorganized the economy of the Duchy of Wurttemburg in Germany. His ideas, however, angered the more conservative members of the Duchy's government and when the Duke of Wurttemburg died in 1737, "Jew" Suss was accused of a number of offences, including stealing state funds. He was found guilty and sentenced to death, but was promised remission if he would abandon the Jewish faith. He refused, and was hanged at Stuttgart.

was a disastrous time for them. But it was to be far more disastrous for the Poles, since the Jews had been practically running the nation in all important walks of life.

In Germany, meanwhile, torn almost to pieces in the Thirty Years War—because the contending nations had used German territory for their battlegrounds—the Jews had been allowed to remain and their conditions had improved greatly. After the war when new states emerged under strong leaders, Jews occupied many high positions even in those states which claimed officially to be discouraging Jews from living there at all.

The eighteenth century saw a slight improvement in toleration for Jews. In Germany they were beginning to be admitted to Universities. In some Italian states Jews were allowed to live outside the ghettos. In Austria in 1781 the Emperor Joseph II abolished the Poll Tax on Jews and said that they need no longer wear the hated yellow badge. Then followed a series of laws aimed at easing the restrictions on Jews generally. For example, they were allowed to open factories, they could send their children to schools, and they could run farms.

Much of the impetus for these reforms came as a result of the work of Moses Mendelssohn, grandfather of the famous composer Felix Mendelssohn. Moses was a scholar with many gifts. He was born in Germany in 1729. In 1763 he won a prize at the Academy of Sciences in Prussia for a brilliant essay and this made him famous. He suddenly found himself acceptable in German society. Rich nobles invited him to their houses. In the meanwhile he kept up writing works in German and in Hebrew, mainly on Jewish law and religion. His influence grew, and through it some of the barriers between the Jews and the Gentiles (non-Jews) began to disappear. It was seen that the differences between them were not irreconcilable. Mendelssohn had Christian friends in various countries who helped towards more toleration of Jews. One was von Dohm who may have been instrumental in persuading the Emperor Joseph of Austria to introduce his reforms.

The Jews in France

In 1789 all Europe, indeed almost the whole known world, was electrified by the news of the outbreak of the French Revolution. This was no ordinary rising, no simple gesture of protest against long-standing ill-treatment. It was an attempt, which proved partly successful, to uproot French society from top to bottom, and begin again. The French revolutionaries were so anxious to break with the past that they renumbered the years starting with 1789, and even changed the names of the months.

The French Revolution was one of the decisive movements of all history and resulted in a new form of government in France which was eventually taken over by Napoleon Bonaparte, who made himself emperor. In some respects he recreated those elements of the old order which the Revolution aimed to get rid of, but he also restructured the law so that most of the injustices could not recur.

Napoleon started off by being good to the Jews. He gave them employment in the army in his earlier conquests. During his campaign in Egypt he

Napoleon's strategy to enlist the aid of Jews from Germany and Russia for his military campaigns was to convene a sanhedrin. The French emperor hoped that the restoration of a Jewish institution, which had ceased to function many hundreds of years before, would focus the loyalties of Jewry on Paris.

promised them a new home in Palestine, encouraging them to join him when he attacked the Sultan of the Ottoman Turkish Empire. But the Jews remembered the help given them by Turkey in the sixteenth century and declined. This angered Napoleon, and he devised a cunning scheme by which to punish the Jews and at the same time make it look as if he was doing them a great favour.

Napoleon summoned leading French Jews to a French sanhedrin. This meeting was supposed to restore the sanhedrin as a regular feature of Jewish life. It was to meet in Paris, and thus establish France as the new world centre for the Jews.

Napoleon's main idea was to win the loyalty of Jews in such lands as Germany, Austria and Poland, so that when he tried to overrun Europe, the Jews in these countries would rise up in his favour. The scheme did not work, partly because the countries involved took care not to aggravate the Jewish communities in their territories.

In retaliation, Napoleon introduced a strict series of laws against the Jews in 1808. They were forbidden to engage in trade except by special permit which was hard to obtain. Debts owing to them by soldiers were cancelled. These and other measures made many Jews poor and also seriously affected the economic health of France.

The Jews only recovered their rights in the time of Louis XVIII, the brother of the executed Louis XVI, who was restored when Napoleon abdicated. Thereafter, for a generation or two they received every encouragement, especially under Napoleon's nephew, Napoleon III (1852-70). In return they invested huge sums of money in French industrial development, and in projects like the railways.

By the end of the century, however, a fresh wave of anti-Jewish feeling was spreading throughout France. It was stirred up by French socialists who apparently believed that the Jews were bent on world domination. Much of this hostility was felt in the army, and it was brought to a head by what was called the Dreyfus Scandal.

The Struggle for Equal Rights

Benjamin Disraeli, Earl of Beaconsfield (1804-81), statesman and novelist. (Mansell Collection).

Baron Lionel de Rothschild, (1808-79), banker and first Jewish M.P. (N. M. Rothschild & Sons)

Baron von Reuter (1816-90), founder of the international news agency, Reuters. (Reuters Library)

Jews in the 19th Century

IN nineteenth century Europe the Jews began at last to obtain those rights to equal treatment that they had been denied intermittently for centuries. They were helped by a general desire for governmental and political reform which spread throughout Europe after the French Revolution. Jews helped these movements for reform everywhere and when reforms were made it was no longer possible to deny Jews equal rights with all other people—or so it was argued. This is one reason why in every constructive movement of the nineteenth century you will find Jews playing an important part. The very founder of communism, Karl Marx, was a Jew from Germany.

We have seen that Restoration France gave the Jews the equality they wanted. In 1830 the movement for the emancipation of the Jews began afresh in Germany and Austria, and over the next fifteen years state after state gave Jews their rights. The same happened in Austria. A temporary halt took place after 1848, the Year of Revolutions, when nearly every nation in Europe rose up against its reigning house or government. Then by 1860 the movement started again. Denmark, Sweden, and Hungary followed the German and Austrian examples. In Italy, which was fighting to win unity among the various states, Jews played a leading part. The leader of the revolt in Venice was a Jew When, in 1870, Italy became a nation, one of the first acts of the new government was to give Jews their rights.

In England the process took some time. Although

Benjamin Disraeli, who was of Jewish birth, was not barred from taking his seat in the House of Commons when he was first elected a member of Parliament in 1837, practising Jews were barred. Lionel de Rothschild was elected several times by the City of London, but was prohibited every time from taking his seat. Not until 1858 was he able to enter the Commons properly and so represent the community to which he had already contributed so much. His son was eventually made an English baron and thus became the first Jew to be created a peer in English history.

The nineteenth century saw the emergence of a large number of distinguished Jews who rose to the very top of their chosen careers. In the financial world we find the first generation of names that have since become very famous—Stern, Oppenheim, Seligman, Sassoon and Goldschmidt. Nathan Meyer Rothschild, whose father had made a lot of money in banking in Frankfort, Germany, came to live in Manchester at the end of the eighteenth century. Within twenty years he had become one of the leading financiers in London, then the richest capital city in the world. He loaned money to governments; he organized the payment of armies; he supported vast schemes of development and business ventures of a social nature; and he patronized the arts. One of his descendants loaned Disraeli the money with which to purchase enough shares in the Suez Canal company, in 1875, to make Britain the majority shareholder, and thus the virtual controller of the then vital waterway.

The Jews excelled in almost every other field. The first manager of a proper news agency was von Reuter (1816-90). Ludwig Mond (1839-1909) introduced the first chemical industry into England which developed into Imperial Chemical Industries (I.C.I.). Adolphe Crémieux, a brilliant lawyer and Minister of Justice in France in 1848, abolished slavery in the French colonies. Heinrich Heine became one of the best known of all German poets. Felix Mendelssohn composed some of the finest music of the nineteenth century.

Adolphe Crémieux (1796-1880), French lawyer, orator and Minister of Justice.

Chaim Nachman Bialik (1873-1943), leading poet of the Hebrew renaissance.

Felix Mendelssohn (1809-47), one of the great classic-romantic German composers. (Mansell Collection)

The Jews in America

ALTHOUGH today the United States of America is probably the least anti-Jewish nation in the world, this has not always been so. The early member states did not immediately grant their Jewish communities equality. The communities were in many cases fairly large, since America had been one of the few places of refuge to which Marrano victims of the Inquisition as well as victims from Germany, Russia and Austria, could flee with safety, if not with equal status.

One of the leading Jews of the early nineteenth century in America was Mordecai Noah (1785-1851), a swashbuckling ex-army officer turned journalist and politician who was descended from a Marrano family. Noah conceived the idea of a new city in America especially for refugee Jews, but when this did not meet with favour he devoted his energies to campaigning for the establishment of a home for Jews in Palestine. The Ottoman empire was declining and the idea was not as far-fetched as it may

In the late 19th-century and early part of the 20th-century thousands of Jewish emigrants arrived in America—most of them fleeing the persecution and restrictions of Czarist Russia and the areas under her influence.

have seemed. Though there was a general lack of enthusiasm from other Jews, Noah's idea became an obsession. In 1837 he actually offered to buy Palestine from the Turks for hard cash, but the ridicule which followed this amazing offer put an end, for a while, to Jewish aspirations for a new home.

How did the Jews fare in the America of mid-nineteenth century? Circumstances in this vast land were very different from those in European countries. Jews who wandered into towns and villages and opened up businesses did not meet the envy of long-entrenched rivals. Their business sense was unequalled in the American frontier, and therefore valuable in all manner of contexts. It is even said that they were the best intermediaries between the white men and the Red Indians.

There was a new wave of anti-Jewish feeling in the 1880's in Europe, especially in Russia. In 1882, the Czar, Alexander II, was assassinated. Immediately some Jews were blamed, and there followed terrible persecutions (called pogroms) by the public of the large population of Russian Jews. Instead of intervening, the Russian government passed a series of very strict anti-Jewish laws, pushing Jews back into the kind of servitude and humiliation they had known several centuries earlier elsewhere in Europe.

Thousands of Jews managed to escape from Russia, and a great percentage made their way to America. It is said that in a little over ten years more than half a million Jewish refugees reached America, and the numbers increased in the early years of the present century. Soon they were employed in every walk of life, enriching the new nation, especially the community of New York which was already America's largest city.

The United States of America had indeed become a second home for Jews. But towards the end of the century a serious move was again made to get a home in Palestine for Jews, and the idea was received with considerable favour in America.

The Beginning of Zionism

An inevitable reaction against the growing amount of liberal government in Europe appeared first in the new Germany. The German people, under the Kaiser and his chancellor, Otto von Bismarck, having obtained unity after winning the Franco-Prussian War of 1870-1, began to believe themselves to be a race apart. To enjoy this belief they were prepared to surrender many of their newly-obtained democratic rights, and as the Jews had been prominent in the movement towards more rights, they now became victims of a new campaign of persecution. This set off a wave of anti-Jewish feeling throughout Europe. In Germany it manifested itself in a fresh series of harsh laws against Jews. They could not go into the army, the civil service, or the professions, without first being baptized as Christians.

In France the anti-Jewish feeling boiled over when the Dreyfus Scandal occurred.

Alfred Dreyfus, a Jew and a captain in the regular army, was arrested in 1894 and tried by court martial for allegedly passing military secrets to Germany. A letter said to have been written by him about the secrets was given as the principal evidence against him. He was convicted and sentenced to life imprisonment on Devil's Island, amid a spate of insults in the press against the Jews in general.

It later transpired that the letter had been written by a Major Esterhazy, who actually walked into the offices of a London newspaper and confessed to the forgery. For a long time the French government refused to re-open the case as too many high ranking people were involved in the plot to convict Dreyfus. Five years later, however, a new government re-tried Dreyfus and although the court again condemned him—despite Esterhazy's confession in London—the President of France pardoned him. The court's

Theodore Herzl, the founder of Zionism, wrote his ideas about founding a nation for Jews in an important book, Der Judenstaat *(The Jewish State), in 1896. He believed that Palestine was the right place for the new homeland.*

The Degradation of Captain Dreyfus. Captain Dreyfus was found guilty of betraying military secrets to the German government. He was sentenced to life imprisonment and stripped of his rank.

Chaim Weizmann (1874-1952) was perhaps the greatest figure in the Zionist movement. He did more than anyone to bring about the creation of the state of Israel, and it was not surprising that he was elected its first President.

verdict was eventually set aside and Dreyfus was exonerated. Out of this terrible injustice arose a new movement, which aimed at setting up a home for Jews in Palestine from whence they had been scattered hundreds of centuries before. It was called the Zionist movement, after Mount Zion in Jerusalem, on which Solomon had built the great Temple.

The leading campaigner for this most natural of aspirations was Theodore Herzl (1860-1904), an Austrian journalist who, after the Dreyfus trial which he had, in fact, attended, became convinced that a home for the Jews was the only real solution to the Jewish problem. Of course not all Jews agreed with him, for many were quite happy to remain in America and Britain.

Herzl discussed the idea at the highest level in many countries. He met the Pope, kings, presidents, and prime ministers, all of whom seemed favourable in principle. The Sultan of Ottoman Turkey was actually prepared to give the Jews the whole of Palestine, but the plan did not materialize. Herzl died in 1904, but the movement lived on.

During the First World War (1914-18) a Jewish chemist of Russian birth, living and working in England, introduced an important development of high explosives that greatly helped the British War effort. His name was Chaim Weizmann and his work came to the notice of the Prime Minister, David Lloyd George.

The Balfour Declaration

CHAIM WEIZMANN tried to persuade Lloyd George to put the weight of Britain's influence behind the Zionist desire for a home in Palestine, and succeeded. In November 1917 the British Foreign Secretary, Arthur Balfour, declared that the British Government favoured the idea in a letter to Lord Rothschild who was one of the leading Jews in England at the time and a champion of Zionism. The letter said:

"His Majesty's Government view with favour the establishment in Palestine of a national home for the Jewish people, and will use their best endeavours to facilitate the achievement of this object, it being clearly understood that nothing shall be done which may prejudice the civil and religious rights of existing non-Jewish communities in Palestine, or the rights and political status enjoyed by Jews in any other country."

The phrase "a national home" was to cause a great deal of trouble ever afterwards, and the proper meaning is still argued about today.

A few months later British and Palestinian forces drove the Ottoman Turks, who had sided with Germany in the First World War, out of Palestine. It seemed as if the Zionist dream was about to be fulfilled.

Unfortunately, promises were also made by other people to Arab peoples living in certain other lands under the banner of the Ottomans. These included undertakings that if the Arabs would rise up against their masters with British military aid they would be granted independence when the Turks were finally defeated.

You will see that there was bound to be trouble if the Jews were given their old land back and the

The Wailing Wall
The Wailing Wall, which is part of the wall around the remains of Solomon's Temple in Jerusalem, is sacred to Jews because it is close to where the Holy of Holies was situated. This was a chamber in the Temple which contained the Ark of the Covenant—the chest in which the tablets of the laws of Moses were kept.

Arabs were promised freedom to live there at the same time. And trouble there was.

The great powers, in this instance, Britain, France and the United States, put Palestine under the protection of Britain as a "mandate", that is, a land whose inhabitants have semi-independence but whose activities are watched over by a supervising power which has ultimate control. A High Commissioner was sent out, Sir Herbert Samuel, one of the most distinguished Jews in Britain. Under his rule thousands of Jews from many parts of the world, but particularly Eastern Europe, came to Palestine to settle. They mingled with Jews whose families had been there for some time.

There was constant friction between the Jews and the Arabs who were allowed to stay there. Riots, often serious ones, broke out on many occasions, and people were killed. There seemed some doubt as to what land the Jews were to have. This was made a little clearer in 1922 when part of Palestine was cut off and allotted to the Emir Abdullah as the kingdom of Transjordan. Almost all of the Jewish settlements were to the west of the river Jordan.

Samuel attempted to make peace between both sides but it could not really work. He set up a Legislative Council consisting of the High Commissioner, ten official members and twelve elected members (ten Arabs and two Jews), but the Arabs boycotted the Council. Samuel then made a great mistake. He appointed as Arab ruler or Mufti, of Jerusalem, a cunning and ruthless politician, Haj Amin, a member of an old Palestinian Arab family. The Mufti proved to be totally unwilling to cooperate either with the Jews or with the British.

Notwithstanding the difficulties, Palestine was fairly quiet for some years. That is not to say there were no disturbances, but such as there were in no way equalled those that were to come. In 1929, however, a small disturbance in Jerusalem beside the Wailing Wall escalated into a series of violent Arab-Jewish riots.

Tragedy and Liberation

Palestine in the 1930's

THE Wailing Wall was, and still is, most sacred to the Jews. It was also part of a holy Arab building. This alone provided grounds for endless bickering and fighting, and it is surprising that serious trouble did not occur long before 1929, when an incident by the Wall sparked off a series of riots all over Palestine in which many Jews and Arabs were killed. It seems the Mufti had goaded Arabs against the Jews because of the Arab resentment over the presence of Jews in Palestine and for fear that the Jews would make the Arabs poor by their superior skill and industry.

The British thereupon investigated the whole economy of Palestine and its future trends, and the report which followed was greeted with a stream of protests from Chaim Weizmann and his colleagues and by influential Jews in Britain. In effect, the Balfour Declaration had come to mean nothing.

The British desperately tried to correct this impression, but that promptly aggravated the Arabs. The next riots were, not surprisingly, directed against the British.

The Jews in Palestine, meanwhile, had been working wonders in their new home. Land hitherto desert, or neglected, or at best poorly cultivated by the Arabs, was recovered and made fertile wherever possible. Many of the resources of civilization were brought to bear to build a modern state. Schools were erected, public works undertaken, factories built and farms managed properly.

This was agreeable for the Jews, but for the Arabs, while it meant a definite increase in their standard of living, it also meant subservience to the Jews, and this is not what they wanted at all. They wanted

Reclaiming the Land
Israel is not a large country and it is not at all rich in natural resources. When Palestine was declared a national home for the Jews in 1917 a great deal of its land was sandy and barren. But the Jews struggled hard to make it fertile. They introduced expensive irrigation schemes and they worked the land, making it yield fruit and grain, sometimes in areas which other nations would have regarded as totally unworkable. Over a million acres have been farmed successfully since 1917, about a third of which are under continual irrigation. In fifteen years Israel increased its export trade of agricultural products tenfold, from about £2m in 1949 to about £22m in 1964. The figures are likely to be somewhat higher since the occupation of parts of the Negev desert and Sinai, where fresh schemes to make the areas fertile are in hand.

Kibbutzim (people who live in the Kibbutz communities) working the land.

the independence which their kinsmen in Iraq, Transjordan and Syria already had, and the only way this could be obtained was by having the Jews expelled from Palestine. Effort after effort was made by many Jewish leaders like Weizmann to come to reasonable terms with the Arabs but the latter would not shift an inch from their demands.

The British tried to assist with another Commission but it was of no avail. Riots went on, and the British government sent in troops, suggesting partition into two states, one for Arabs and one for Jews. Some Jews would have accepted this, including Weizmann. The German terror (*See* page 86) had begun and the number of refugees coming to Palestine had started to increase rapidly. Weizmann felt, in the circumstances, that half a state was better than no state at all.

The Arabs on their part were terrified by the pressures building up in Palestine and fighting broke out again. British troops were again used to put them down. Then the British government proposed limiting Jewish immigration to about 15,000 people a year. This was not what the Balfour Declaration had promised. The Jews were dismayed, but the Arabs were still dissatisfied. They wanted to see the end of immigration and the beginning of another exodus.

The outbreak of war in 1939 between Britain and Germany, which developed into World War II, detracted attention from the Palestinian problem. Meanwhile a critical stage in Jewish history occurred when Hitler came to power in 1933.

Laying pipeline in the Negev desert to irrigate the land for crop growing.

The Greatest Crime in History

The anti-Jewish feeling that had returned in Germany in the time of Bismarck (*See* page 80) never really died out. But in 1933 few could have foreseen the horrible extent of the unspeakable crimes the Germans were to commit against the Jews in the next twelve years.

Hitler, an Austrian-born house painter who became a political agitator in Germany after the First World War, was actively anti-Jewish when a young man in Vienna. Part of his post-war political programme, which in the hard times in Germany in the 1920's won enormous support, was the suppression of the Jews. Hitler contrived to blame Jewish influence for every one of Germany's misfortunes.

When at last in 1933, the president invited him to become chancellor, the fate of millions of Jews was sealed.

The largest community of Jews in Poland in 1939 was in the Warsaw ghetto. The population there was about 350,000. When German forces over-ran Poland in September 1939, the ghetto was surrounded by eight-foot-high concrete walls. Some time later orders were issued by Hitler for the deportation of the inhabitants to death camps.

From 1933 to 1938 the persecutions were limited to German Jews and from 1938 to 1939, Austrians and Czechoslovakians also became victims. Special concentration camps were set up all over Germany into which thousands of Jews of every walk of life were herded, without trial. Fortunes were seized, houses looted and burned, possessions smashed, people beaten up and insulted in the streets. Many escaped the country, and among these was Albert Einstein, the originator of the theory of relativity, and one of the greatest theoretical physicists of all time.

In September 1939 Europe was at war. By the summer of 1940 Hitler's aggressive policies, extremely well carried out by the most efficient military machine in world history, had resulted in the subjection of most of Europe. Poland, France, Belgium, Holland, Norway and Denmark, were all in his power. In 1941 he attacked and swiftly overran nearly a million square miles of Russia. Yugoslavia and Greece had already fallen.

Then, almost the whole Jewish population of this vast area of land was arrested and imprisoned, brutally assaulted, and murdered in countless instances. The numbers ran into many millions. There were too many to handle, to keep alive in the camps. So Hitler and his henchmen devised means—gas ovens, huge, cavernous chambers of death—which were capable of disposing of hundreds of human beings at a time with one switch of the taps.

Horrible to relate, the Jews of occupied Europe were almost extirpated, cut down from 9,000,000 to less than 3,000,000, about half the entire Jewish population of the whole world. The majority of these were Polish—3,000,000 out of 3,500,000 of them perished. The Jews left in Europe were poor, starving and homeless. Many of them found their way to Palestine after 1945 but many more were lost forever.

It is impossible to overstate the enormity of this frightful crime. No words can begin to describe what so many deaths meant not only to the Jewish race but also to civilized people all over the world.

The Creation of the State of Israel

IN the Second World War (1939-45) thousands of Jews in Palestine volunteered to fight with the Allies, Great Britain, France and the U.S.A. In 1944 a special Jewish Brigade was formed at the insistence of Winston Churchill, the British war leader, and acquitted itself with great gallantry.

In Palestine, immigrants had been filtering in throughout the war. As persecution by the Germans got worse, more and more Jews fled to Palestine. The British government, however, had been trying to limit immigration to about 15,000 persons a year, so a very explosive situation arose. The Jews in Palestine were determined not only to see the Balfour Declaration adhered to, but also to help their compatriots driven out of Nazi Germany. It was not long before one or two organizations of armed terrorists were formed to try to enforce the Jewish demands. One was the Irgun Tzvai Leumi (National Military Organization), known as the Irgun, and another was a gang led by Abraham Stern called the Stern gang. Both organizations were anti-British. Stern was killed by British military police in 1942, but his gang was not broken up. By 1944 both gangs were working more or less together.

It was clear that the Jews would not get their state without a fight. So they had to have arms. These were obtained by daring raids on British military depots.

Chaim Weizmann did not like this violence at all. But many Jews believed it to be necessary. One was David Ben-Gurion, a Polish-born Jew who had emigrated to Palestine in 1906 and who had been the equivalent of the general secretary of the Trades Union Congress. He was a different kind of person from the kindly and charming

Kibbutz
A kibbutz is an almost unique form of social organization. It is a group of people working together on one farm, who share the produce among each other. These people also organize their own medical services, build their own homes and run their own schools. The children are brought up in a communal nursery.

Ben-Gurion (b. 1886) was the first prime minister of Israel, and he held office for five years. He retired, but took office again, in 1955, for eight more years. He has played a dominant part in the development of Israel and is now the country's most respected "elder statesman".

Weizmann, though both were men of determination. Ben-Gurion understandably had given up hope of any agreement with the British. The British Foreign Secretary in 1917 had promised the Jews a home; since then succeeding statesmen had shilly-shallied over the matter, trying to get out of the commitment.

The British made the mistake of trying to organize Palestine as a bi-national state. So from 1945 to 1948 the Irgun and Stern organizations kept up their acts of terrorism while Britain and other nations floundered about in conference after conference trying to find a solution. The Arabs, still led by the Mufti, declared that if partition was tried, they would go to war at once. Finally, the British decided to get out of Palestine in 1948, and on 13 May the last High Commissioner left Haifa.

The very next morning the leading Jews, constituting what was called the National Council, whose chairman was Ben-Gurion, declared the State of Israel a new and independent nation. Part of the proclamation, which was read by Ben-Gurion, said: "The state will promote the development of the country for all its inhabitants, will be based on the precepts of liberty, justice and peace taught by the Hebrew prophets, will uphold full social and political equality for all its citizens without distinction of race, creed or sex."

Ben-Gurion became the first prime minister of Israel. The first president was Dr. Chaim Weizmann. For him a forty-year-old dream had come true.

The Arab states—Egypt, Syria and Jordan—were already hammering at Israel's borders, but the Jewish forces held them all at bay. The United Nations Organization intervened and sent Count Bernadotte as peacemaker. But peace did not come, and Bernadotte was assassinated. The Israeli army, fighting for the very existence of the new state, pushed the Arabs back into their own territories. In February 1949 the Jews provisionally agreed new boundaries with Egypt, Lebanon, Jordan and Syria, but the old city of Jerusalem was halved between Israel and Jordan.

War with the Arabs

THE independent state of Israel had come about at last. The Israelis wanted very much to settle down and get on with the business of developing the state. But their Arab neighbours were not disposed to let them. They refused to recognize Israel as a state, despite the fact that the United Nations Organization had done so, and they would not accept the fact that they had been beaten in the field of battle by a collection of "wandering infidels". Instead, the Arabs kept up a permanent state of tension all along the borders of Israel, continually raiding towns and kibbutzim, and meeting retaliation from the Israelis.

After the declaration of 15 May the immigration rate increased very quickly. Although it gave rise to serious problems of accommodation, employment, housing, welfare and money, there were no more restrictions by foreign powers. Jews from everywhere were welcomed like long lost relatives. They came from the Yemen, Iraq, Turkey, Morocco, Tunisia, Egypt, and they also came from Europe. From 1949 to 1951 over 300,000 immigrants came in.

Where was the money to house, feed and employ them to come from? The government decided to press a claim for compensation from Germany for the crimes of Hitler and the Nazis. While no money on earth could begin to compensate for so many deaths, an arbitrary sum was fixed—$1,500,000,000. After much difficulty about half this amount was obtained. In addition huge sums were raised by subscription in the United States, always quick to respond generously to appeals for money by oppressed peoples.

With this help and with their own skills the Israelis modernized their country.

By 1956 the Arab attacks along the borders,

Israeli troops make preparations to resist attack along the borders of their country.

sponsored mainly by Egypt under President Nasser, had become so irritating that the Israeli government decided to attack Egypt. In a lightning campaign the Israeli army overran the whole Sinai peninsula and reached the Suez Canal. Britain and France intervened by sending expeditionary forces into the Suez Canal zone, but in so doing earned the condemnation of the world, including the U.S.A. World opinion forced Britain and France to withdraw, causing the Israelis to retire as well and a United Nations force was stationed between Israeli and Egyptian territory in Gaza to keep the peace.

For ten years Israel and the Arab world remained at loggerheads. While open war was not declared, border fighting went on.

Russia, with its long history of hostility to Jews and its age-old policy of trying to dominate the Middle East, supported the Arabs, especially the shaky regime of Gamal Nasser in Egypt. Vast military reinforcements were poured in and these threatened the security of Israel, but as long as the U.N. force was in Gaza there was peace.

The Struggle to Preserve Nationhood

IN May 1967 Nasser demanded that the U.N. force be withdrawn from Gaza. To the astonishment of many people this world body complied. Israel was left to its fate, for the Arabs made no secret of their intention to crush Israel and kill off the inhabitants.

The government had been led for a while by Levi Eshkol, the prime minister, essentially a man of peace and compromise. But the Arabs were in no mood for compromise, and a more decisive and militant leadership was needed. So Eshkol had to reform his government. This time it included the popular Moshe Dayan, brilliant victor of the 1956 Sinai campaign, who was made Minister of Defence.

The maps above show Israel in 1960 and Israel and the occupied territories after the "Six Day War" of 1967. (UPI)

Below: *General Moshe Dayan with Mrs. Golda Meir.* Below right: *Israeli flags wave over the Negev desert.*

On June 5, 1967, the fighting started.

The Israel armies were successful everywhere. In only four days they crushed the Egyptian army in the Sinai desert and drove it back across the Suez Canal. Then the Israelis took up positions along the east bank of the canal from which they have not since moved. Later, another army scoured across all that part of Jordan in Palestine west of the river Jordan and captured the sacred city of Jerusalem. Every man in the conquering army went to the Wailing Wall to pray.

By Monday June 13 the fighting was over. Although the Arabs were tactically defeated in the field a cease-fire was arranged by the U.N.

The Israeli army had shown itself one to be reckoned with. Although heavily outnumbered it proved invincible.

Sad to relate, in very recent years the story of Israel has been like that of the previous nineteen years. The border raids continue, the tension remains, the angry words pour out from the Arab leaders. And Israel has another problem. There are many Palestinian Arab refugees within her borders.

In the domestic sphere, however, Israel is making great strides. Under the prime minister Mrs. Golda Meir, once secretary-general of the Labour Party, Israel's development is gathering momentum.

Israel is not yet a land to which all Jews in the world are attracted. Possibly it never will be. But it must be the wish of civilized people everywhere, that when Jews emigrate to Israel they do so always by choice. Have the days of their tribulations at last come to an end?

Index

Aaron of Lincoln, 54
Abraham, 10, *10*, 11
Abulafia, Samuel, 60
Ahab, *24*, 25
Alexander the Great, 29
Antiochus IV, 30-1
Arabs, 82-5, 88-9, 90-2
Aristobulus II, 32, 33
Ark of the Covenant, *see* Torah
Ashkenazim, 65
Austria, 73, 76
Assyria and Assyrians, 25, 26, *26*
Auto da Fé, *60*

Babylon and Babylonians, 26-7, 28
Balfour Declaration, the, 82
Bar Mitzvah, 65, *69*
Ben-Gurion, David, 88, *89*
Bernadotte, Count, 89
Beth Horon, Battle of, *40*, 41
Bialik, Chaim, 77
Black Death, the, 57
Brazil, 68
Bulan, 47

Canaan, 10, 12, 16-17
Christianity, 39
Claudius, Emperor, 40, 41
Clermont, 52
Columbus, Christopher, 66-7
Constantine, Emperor, 39, 45
Crémieux, Adolphe, 77
Cromwell, Oliver, 69
Crusades, the, 50, *50*, 52-3
Cyrus the Great   27

Darius, King, 28
David, King, *20*, 20-22
Dayan, Moshe, 92, *92*
Diaspora, the, 45, *46*
Dietary laws, *16*
Disraeli, Benjamin, *76*, 77
Dreyfus, Alfred, 75, 80-1, *81*

Edward I, King, 55, 57
Egypt, 12-15; plagues of, 14
Einstein, Albert, 87
Elisha, 24
England, English, 54-5, 69, 77
Eshkol, Levi, 91
Esterhazy, Major, 80
Esther, *29*; Scroll of, *28*
Exodus, the, 14, *15*

Fertile Crescent, the, 10, *11* (map)
Florus, 41
France and French, 74-5

Galilee, 33, 41, 42, 44
Gallus, *40*, 41
Gama, Vasco da, 66
Gamaliel II, 44, *44*, 45
Gaza strip, 91
Germany and Germans, 73, 76, 80, 86-7
Ghettos, the, 62-3
Granada, 49
Greece and Greeks, 29
Hanukkah, 31
Hasdai ibn Shaprut, 48, *48*
Heine, Heinrich, 77
Henry II of France, 68
Henry III, King, 55, 57
Herod Agrippa, 40-1, *40*
Herod Antipas, 34
Herod the Great, 34, *35*

Hertzl, Theodore, *80*, 80
Hillel, 36, *36*, 38
Hitler, Adolf, 86-7
Holland and the Dutch, 67-9
House of Ivory, the, *24*
Hyksos, 13
Hyrcanus II, 32, 33, 34, 35
Hyrcanus, John, 32

Idumeans, 42
Innocent III, Pope, 56
Inquisition, the, 60-1
Irgun, 88, 89
Islam 46 ff
Isaac, 11
Israel, State of, 88-92
Israelites, 11, 12-15, 17, 18, 21, 24, 26, 27

Jacob, 11
Jerusalem, *21*, 22, 24, 28, 33, *42*, 42-43, 50, 56
Jesus of Nazareth, 37-9, *38*
Jezebel, *24*, 25
Joseph, 12
Joseph, ben Mattathias, (Josephus Flavius), 42
Judah, 24, 26-8
Judah ha Levi, 51
Judah of Galilee, 36, *36*
Judah the Maccabee, 30-1
Judea, 31-3, 36, 40, 41, 44, 45
Julian the Apostate, 45
Julius Caesar, 34

Khazars, 47
Kibbutzim, *85*, 89

Land reclamation, *84*
Lloyd George, David, 81, 82

Maccabaeus, Jonathan, 31
Maccabaeus, Simon, 31
Maccabees, the, 30-1
Maimonides (Moses ben Maimon), 51, *51*, 71
Marranos, 60, 66-7, 68-9
Marx, Karl, 76
Mattathias, 30
Meir, Mrs. Golda, 92, *92*
Menasseh ben Israel, 69, *69*
Mendelssohn, Felix, 77, *77*
Mendelssohn, Moses, 72, 73
Menelaus, 30
Menorah, *23*
Mezuzah, *54*
Mohammed, 47
Mond, Ludwig, 77
Moses, 14-15, 16
Mufti, the, 83, 84, 89

Nachmanides, 59
Napoleon, 74-5
Nasi, Gracia, *64*
Nasi, Joseph, 65
Nasis *see* Patriarchs
Nasser, President, 91-2
Nebuchadnezzar II, 26, 27
Negev desert, *85*
Nero, Emperor, 42
Noah, Mordecai, 78, *78*
Nunez, Maria, 67

Omri, 25
Oppenheimer, Joseph, 72

Passover, the, 14, *15*, 59
Patriarchs, the, 44-5
Paul (Saul of Tarsus), 39

Paul IV, Pope, 62
Persecutions, 52-7
Persia and Persians, 27, 28-9
Pharisees, 32, 33, 38
Pharaohs, the, 13, 14
Philistines, *17*, 20, 21
Pilate, Pontius, 38
Poland and Poles, 59, 72
Pompey, (Gnaeus Pompeius Magnus), 33, 34
Prophets, the, 25
Ptolemy, 30
Purim, *29*

Rameses II, 14, *14*
Reuter, Baron von, *76*, 77
Richard I, King, 55
Rome and Romans, 30, 32-45
Rothschild, Lionel de, *76*, 77
Russia, 72, 79

Sadducees, 32, 33, 38
Saladin, 51
Samaria and Samaritans, 28, 42
Samuel, 18, *18*, 20
Samuel, ibn Nagrela, 49
Samuel, Sir Herbert, 83
Sanhedrin, *35*
Sarah, *10*
Sargon II, 26, *26*
Saul, King, *18*, 19, *19*, 20
Seleucus and Seleucids, 30
Selim II, Sultan of Turkey, 65
Septuagint, the, 29
Shofar, the, *70*
Solomon, King, 22-3
Solomon ibn Gabirol, 51
Spain and Spaniards, 48-9, 58-9, 60-1
Spinoza, Baruch de, 70-1
Stern Gang, the, 88, 89
Stuyvesant, Peter, 68
Suez Canal, 77, 91
Sukkoth (Feast of the Tabernacles), *12*
Suleiman the Magnificent, 65
Sumer, 10
Suss, Jew, *see* Oppenheimer
Synagogues, *49*, *53*, 70
Syria and Syrians, 10, 29, 30

Talmud, the, 49, *55*
Temple, the, 22, *22*, 43
Ten Commandments, the, 15, 16 53
Titus, 42, 43
Torah, the, 15, *18*, 25, 46
Torquemada, Tomas de, *61*
Turkey and Turks, 50, 52, 64-5, 75 81-82

United States of America, 78-9, 90
Ur, 10
Urban II, Pope, 52, *52*

Venice, 62, 76
Vespasian, Emperor, 42, 43

Wailing Wall, the, *83*, 83-4, 92
Warsaw ghetto, *86*
Weizmann, Chaim, 81-2, 84, 85, 88, 89

Yom Kippur, *70*

Zacuto, Abraham, 66
Zacutus Lusitanus, *68*
Zealots, 35, 37, 41
Zionism, 80-1

Figures in italic refer to illustrations

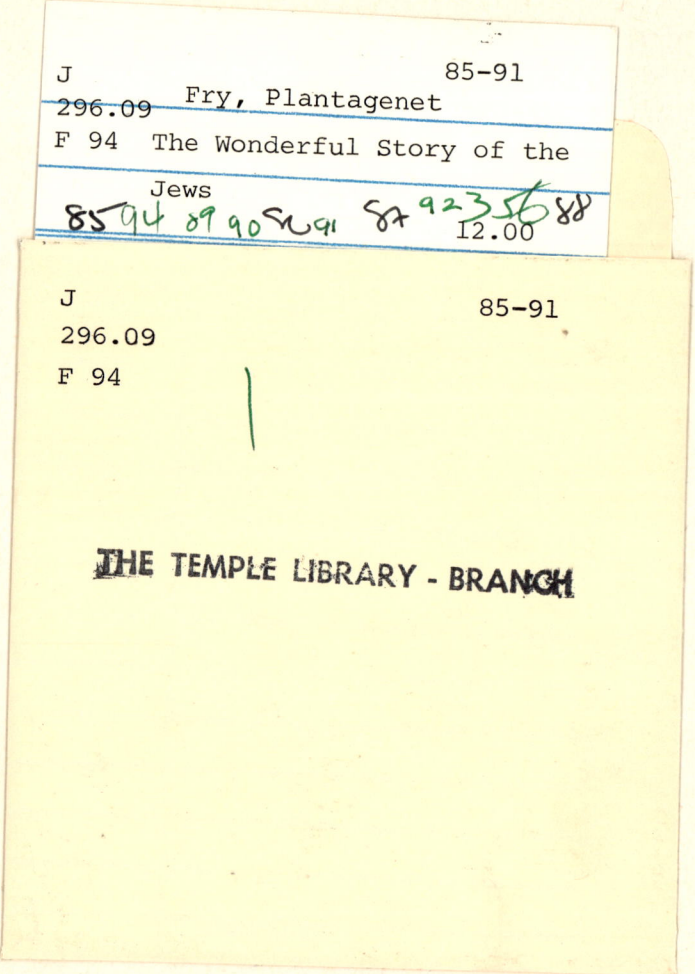

Acknowledgements
The publishers wish to thank the following for illustrative material and for their kind help in providing information and research facilities: the American Jewish Historical Society; the British Museum, Department of Manuscripts; Jacob Gewirtz; the Israel Government Tourist Office; the Staff of the Jewish Chronicle; the Jewish Memorial Council; the Joint Palestine Appeal; the Mansell Collection; the Public Record Office; Radio Times Hulton Picture Library; Reuters Limited; N. M. Rothschild & Sons Limited; Spink's; United Press International Inc. The publishers also wish to thank the following for original illustrations: Gordon King, the Tudor Art Agency Ltd, Jennifer Antoine and Gay Creasey.